BLACK MAN GO HOME!

By D. Raymond Price

ISBN: 979-8-218-89770-3

PRICE HOUSE PUBLISHING

Printed in the United States of America

DEDICATION

This book is dedicated to:

The Black men who were never taught how to be whole,
yet were still expected to lead.

To the fathers who were removed, silenced, incarcerated, or
erased—
not because they did not love their families,
but because the system made their presence illegal.

To the sons who inherited confusion instead of instruction.

And to the men who are brave enough to look backward
so they can finally move forward.

EPIGRAPH

"A people without the knowledge of their past history,
origin and culture are like a tree without roots."
— Marcus Garvey

AUTHOR'S NOTE

This book is written at the intersection of documented history, policy analysis, and lived experience.

While *BLACK MAN GO HOME!* draws from my own life and observations, it is not a memoir. Individual experiences are included only where they illuminate broader patterns created by law, economics, and social design. The primary focus of this work is structural—not personal—and the conclusions reached are supported by historical record, public policy, and observable outcomes across generations.

Some names, dialogue, and identifying details have been altered or generalized where necessary. This was done to protect privacy, preserve narrative flow, and prevent distraction from the systems being examined. These changes do not alter the substance, accuracy, or intent of the arguments presented.

This book does not attempt to catalogue every event, law, or policy that has affected Black men in America. Instead, it traces clear throughlines—from pre-colonial African social structures, through enslavement, Jim Crow, and modern policy frameworks—to demonstrate how manhood, leadership, family continuity, and economic stability were deliberately interrupted and managed over time.

Where claims are made about policy, enforcement, or institutional behavior, they are grounded in historical documentation, legal precedent, or widely acknowledged outcomes. Where interpretation is required, it is stated plainly as analysis—not conjecture. This book does not rely on exaggeration, speculation, or emotional appeal to make its case.

BLACK MAN GO HOME! is not written to indict individual people, nor to absolve individual responsibility. It is written to establish context. Responsibility cannot be discussed honestly without first acknowledging the conditions under which behavior developed.

This work may challenge familiar narratives. It may unsettle comfortable explanations. That is intentional. Comfort has never been the metric of truth.

The goal of this book is not consensus.
It is clarity.

Once clarity exists, meaningful responsibility—personal and collective—can finally begin.

TABLE OF CONTENTS

Introduction
Before America Knew My Name

SECTION I — THE HISTORY
The Village, The Breaking, and The Survival of the Black Man

SECTION II — THE PERSONAL
Forgiveness — From My Perspective

INTRODUCTION

Before America Knew My Name

Before America knew my name,
it knew my body.

It knew my labor before it ever acknowledged my humanity.
It knew my strength before it ever considered my mind.
It knew my usefulness long before it cared about my wholeness.

Before America knew my name, it decided what I was allowed to
be.

This book is not an apology.
It is not a complaint.
It is not a demand for sympathy.

It is an explanation that Black men in America are often spoken
about as if we appeared fully broken—
as if dysfunction was our origin instead of our interruption.

We are discussed as statistics, headlines, and even
cautionary tales.
Rarely are we traced backward.

Rarely does anyone ask *how* a people known for structure,
discipline, invention, protection, and spiritual order became
synonymous with absence, incarceration, emotional distance, and
fracture.

This book asks that question without flinching.

What you are holding is not just history.
It is not a memoir.

It is a map.

A map that connects villages to plantations.
Plantations to policies.

Policies to prisons.
Prisons to living rooms where sons grew up without fathers
and men learned how to survive without ever learning how to be
whole.

I am not writing as an outsider looking in.
I am writing as a man who inherited this silence
and spent years mistaking survival for identity.

I was not taught manhood.
I was taught endurance.

I was not shown how to lead.
I was shown how to navigate chaos.

I was not given a blueprint.
I was given instincts—sharp enough to survive,
but not refined enough to build legacy.

And yet, like many Black men, I was still expected to know how
to love, provide, protect, and lead without ever being taught how
any of that works.

This book does not ask you to excuse Black men.
It asks you to understand them.

Understanding is not forgiveness.
Understanding is not agreement.

Understanding is responsibility.

Because once we see the full structure—
once we recognize the systems, the fractures, the intentional removals—
we are no longer allowed to pretend we don't know why things are the way they are.

This book is written for Black men first.

Not to shame us.
Not to absolve us.

But to ground us.

To educate even us.

To remind us that we did not begin at the bottom,
and that survival—while necessary—was never meant to be the destination.

Going home does not mean going backward.
It means returning to responsibility.

This history created generations of men who were never taught how to be whole.

Men who learned how to hustle before they learned how to heal.
Men who learned how to endure before they learned how to lead.
Men who were taught what to avoid, but not what to build.

I am one of those men.

And this is where the story begins.

THE HISTORY

The Village, The Breaking, and The Survival of the Black Man

CHAPTER 1

Before We Were Broken

The African Blueprint of Manhood

Before the Black man was ever introduced to chains,
he was introduced to structure.

This is the part of the story that is rarely examined honestly,
because understanding where Black men began forces an
admission about how deliberate the destruction had to be. You
do not dismantle chaos. You dismantle structure.

Long before European ships touched African shores, African
societies were not random, primitive, or disorganized. They were
organized civilizations built on systems of accountability,
hierarchy, responsibility, and discipline. These were not perfect
societies, but they were intentional ones. And the Black male
was never designed to move through life without direction.

Across West and Central Africa—among the Yoruba, Igbo,
Akan, Mandinka, Wolof, and countless other nations—manhood
was not something a boy claimed. It was something he was
granted after observation, correction, testing, and proof.

A boy was never left to raise himself.

From early childhood, Black boys were watched by men who
were not their biological fathers but still held responsibility over
them. This was not community as a slogan. It was community as
obligation. A man was considered dishonorable if he watched a
boy grow without guidance and said nothing.

Many African societies operated under structured age-grade systems. These were not symbolic or ceremonial. They were developmental roadmaps. Boys moved through stages of life together under the supervision of elder men who were accountable for shaping temperament, discipline, emotional regulation, sexual responsibility, and restraint.

A boy was taught how to speak to elders.
How to sit in the presence of men.
How to listen before he spoke.

Silence was not weakness.
Silence was training.

You learned before you led.

By adolescence, boys entered separation training. This was not trauma. It was preparation. They were temporarily removed from the comfort of childhood and introduced to teaching spaces where they learned community law, family responsibility, endurance, self-control, and restraint.

In some societies, this took the form of formal initiation rites. Western writers often reduce these rites to superstition or brutality, but they were psychological systems. They marked the death of the child identity and the birth of the man. A boy was not considered a man because of size, age, or physical ability. He was considered a man when the community judged him capable of carrying the weight of other people's lives.

Emotional discipline was considered masculine power.
Not emotional absence.
Not suppression.
Regulation.

A man was expected to know pain without becoming ruled by it. He was taught to hold emotion, not flee from it. Not to explode. Not to bury it. To master it.

This matters, because the modern world teaches Black men that pain must either be hidden or discharged violently. That was never the original design.

The African man was not taught to dominate his household through fear. He was taught to stabilize it through structure. The expectation was not control. The expectation was responsibility. If a man failed, the household suffered. If the household suffered, the village suffered. And when the village suffered, men were held accountable.

There were consequences for men who abused women. Consequences for men who neglected children. Consequences for men who failed their duties.

Men were not worshiped. They were weighed.

Masculinity was measured by the ability to serve something larger than self.

Strength was not for ego. The body was not for chaos. The voice was not for noise.

A man existed to protect stability.

When famine came, men were expected to endure hunger first. When war threatened, men were expected to stand first. When conflict arose, men were expected to speak last and think first.

This was not romance.
This was design.

And that design is precisely why the destruction had to be so thorough.

America did not inherit a broken Black man.
America captured a structured one.

The men forced onto slave ships were often warriors, farmers, leaders, fathers, ritual guides, and protectors. European traders did not accidentally select the strongest among us. They targeted them. Strong men who could work, endure, survive, organize, and rebuild.

That matters.

Because when you capture men trained for responsibility, discipline, and leadership, you cannot simply shackle their bodies. Those men will organize. They will resist. They will rebuild. So, the identity had to be dismantled first.

This is why breaking came before labor.

This is why names were stripped.
Languages forbidden.
Lineage severed.
Families split deliberately.

You cannot fully enslave a man who still knows who he is.

So, the first objective was not physical enslavement.
It was psychological interruption.

Remove the elders.
Destroy the village.
Disrupt the transfer of manhood.

A man without context is easier to redefine.
A man without memory is easier to repurpose.

What followed was not the introduction of brutality—violence exists in every society—but the removal of continuity. The intentional erasure of what connected Black men to themselves and to one another.

This is the part of the story rarely told without distortion.

Black men were not "naturally" aggressive, irresponsible, or emotionally detached. Those traits emerged later as adaptations to environments designed to punish leadership, criminalize authority, and reward silence.

Before we were broken, we were built.

And that distinction matters, because you cannot diagnose damage accurately unless you understand what was damaged.

This chapter is not about longing for a romantic past. It establishes baseline reality. You cannot understand what happened to Black men in America unless you acknowledge that we were not created in the conditions we were forced to survive.

We were interrupted.

Every chapter that follows is the story of that interruption—how it evolved, how it adapted, and how its consequences are still being lived out in real time.

Before America knew my name,
it knew exactly what it was dismantling.

CHAPTER 2

Manhood Before America

Manhood, before America, was not a performance.

It was not loud.
It was not insecure.
It was not something a man had to announce, posture, or prove through dominance, violence, or accumulation.

It was something he was prepared for.

In many African societies, masculinity was treated as a responsibility that carried weight, consequence, and expectation. A man was not simply stronger than others; he was expected to use that strength wisely. His power existed in service of stability—not ego, not control, and not personal gratification.

Manhood began with discipline.

A boy was taught early that his impulses were not his identity. Desire was not command. Anger was not authority. He learned restraint before he learned force, patience before privilege. These were not abstract virtues or moral slogans. They were survival tools for the community.

A man who could not govern himself could not be trusted to govern anything else.

Rites of passage formalized this understanding. They were not symbolic ceremonies meant to inflate confidence or provide cultural theater. They were designed to strip a boy of comfort, expose him to hardship, and return him to the community changed—accountable not only to himself, but to others.

During these rites, boys were separated from women and children not out of disrespect, but out of preparation. They were taught by men who had already endured what they were about to face. Elders spoke plainly. There was no illusion and no sugarcoating. Manhood was not promised as ease; it was framed honestly—as burden, responsibility, and obligation.

A man learned what it meant to protect without possession.
To provide without control.
To lead without domination.

He learned that strength without wisdom was dangerous—not admirable.

This distinction matters, because modern conversations around masculinity often confuse power with presence. Before America, a man's presence was measured by how stable his environment was when he entered and how intact it remained when he left.

If his family was fed, safe, and supported, he was respected.
If his community thrived, he was trusted.
If he abused his authority, he was corrected.

Masculinity was communal, not individualistic.

No man stood alone. No man succeeded alone. And no man failed alone either. Accountability was collective. When a man fell short, it reflected on those who taught him—and those men were expected to intervene.

This structure did not eliminate conflict, jealousy, or ambition. It contextualized them. A man was allowed to compete, but not at the expense of the village. Advancement was encouraged, but not if it destabilized others.

There was an understanding that a man's greatness was inseparable from the health of his people.

Contrast that with what would come later.

America would introduce a version of masculinity stripped of instruction and obsessed with outcome. A version where power was disconnected from responsibility. Where men were expected to perform strength without ever being taught how to carry it.

Before that disruption, manhood was not something a man discovered on his own. It was something he was walked into deliberately.

Elders mattered.

Older men did not retreat from younger ones. They were not distant, silent, or absent. They were present, visible, and involved. They corrected boys publicly and privately. They modeled behavior consistently. There was no confusion about what a man looked like, sounded like, or stood for.

A boy knew who to imitate because the examples were clear.

This clarity is precisely what made the later destruction so effective.

When those systems were removed—when elders were killed, displaced, criminalized, or stripped of authority—boys were left with instincts but no instruction. Strength without structure becomes volatility. Desire without discipline becomes chaos.

Manhood without mentorship does not disappear.

It mutates.

That mutation would later be mislabeled as pathology.
But it began as absence.

Before America, masculinity was not criminalized. It was cultivated. It was tied to land, lineage, and legacy. A man knew that his life extended beyond himself—into his children, his people, and his memory.

This is why the removal of Black male authority was never incidental. It was strategic. You do not need to destroy a people outright if you can interrupt the transfer of manhood.

If boys are never formally taught what it means to be men, they will create substitutes.
If those substitutes are born in trauma, they will reflect trauma. And if those reflections are punished instead of understood, the cycle deepens.

Before America, manhood had a beginning, a process, and a confirmation.

After America, it would become something Black men were expected to figure out alone—while being punished for getting it wrong.

That contradiction is not accidental.

It is foundational.

CHAPTER 3

The Village as Blueprint

The village was not just a place.

It was a system.

Before America, survival was not an individual project. It was communal by design. No man was expected to raise himself, protect himself, or define himself alone. Isolation was understood as dangerous—not empowering.

A man's role inside the village was clear, not because it was rigid, but because it was reinforced from every direction.

Children did not belong only to their parents. They belonged to the community. When a boy mis stepped, correction did not come solely from his father. Any man with standing had both the right and the obligation to intervene. This was not intrusion.

It was responsibility.

The phrase "it takes a village" is often repeated today without understanding what it actually meant.

It meant accountability without ego.
Correction without humiliation.
Protection without possession.
Shared responsibility without ambiguity.

A man could not disappear from his obligations without consequence. Absence was not normalized. Withdrawal was not excused. If a man failed to provide, to teach, or to protect, it was addressed—not ignored.

Masculinity thrives in environments where expectations are clear and consistently enforced.

The village provided that clarity.

Young boys grew up watching men work—not only for pay, but for purpose. Labor was visible. Contribution was tangible. A boy could see how food reached the table, how disputes were resolved, and how decisions were made.

Manhood was learned by proximity.

A boy learned how to speak by listening.
How to carry himself by observing.
How to regulate emotion by watching older men navigate conflict.

There was no mystery to what a man was supposed to become.

The village also protected against extremes. A boy who was too aggressive was tempered. A boy who was withdrawn was drawn out. A boy who was gifted was guided. Individual traits were shaped in ways that benefited the whole.

The village did not erase individuality.

It contextualized it.

Contrast that with environments where boys are raised without male visibility, without correction, without guidance—and then blamed for improvising identities from whatever fragments they can find.

The village understood something modern systems often ignore:

You cannot punish behavior you never taught someone how to replace.

Leadership inside the village was layered. Elders held wisdom. Warriors provided protection. Providers ensured survival. Spiritual leaders anchored meaning. Each role reinforced the others.

No single man carried everything alone.

This prevented burnout, ego inflation, and collapse.

When one man fell, others stepped in. When one man succeeded, it elevated the group. Wealth was not hoarded as proof of superiority. It was circulated as proof of responsibility.

Legacy mattered more than status.

This is why the destruction of the village was the true crime— not merely the enslavement of bodies, but the dismantling of systems that produced balanced men.

When African men were captured, they were not only removed from their homeland. They were removed from feedback loops. They were stripped of mirrors that reflected who they were and who they were becoming.

On plantations, there would be no village—only hierarchy.
No collective accountability—only punishment.
No layered leadership—only domination and fear.

The village was replaced with isolation by design.

Men were separated from men who could correct them. Boys were separated from men who could guide them. Families were fragmented to prevent continuity. What remained was survival stripped of structure.

And survival without structure always produces distortion.

The village had been the blueprint.

Its removal was the sabotage.

Everything that follows in this book traces back to this rupture— the moment when community was replaced with control, and men were expected to function without the systems that had once made manhood sustainable.

CHAPTER 4

Brutality as Control

Brutality was not a reaction to slavery.

It was the foundation of it.

Before Black men ever reached a plantation—before they were sent into fields, before labor could be organized or extracted—control had to be established. Work was never the first objective.

Submission was.

The system understood a simple truth: no economy can function on the backs of men who still believe they belong to themselves. A man who sees himself as sovereign cannot be exploited at scale. His compliance must be manufactured before his labor can be trusted.

That manufacturing began immediately.

Breaking Comes Before Labor

Violence did not begin in the fields.

It began before arrival.

From capture through confinement and transport, Black men were subjected to conditions designed to overwhelm identity and fracture resistance. Shackling, starvation, beatings, forced confinement, sexual violence, and public death were not excesses or accidents. They were preparation.

The Middle Passage was not merely transportation. It was a conditioning environment. Men were packed into darkness, deprived of orientation, stripped of privacy, and surrounded by death. Survival itself became arbitrary. Strength offered no protection. Intelligence offered no escape.

By the time a man reached American soil, the goal was no longer to test obedience.

It was to ensure resistance had already been punished out of him.

The breaking had to occur before labor could be trusted.

The Erasure of Name

One of the first acts of control was not physical.

It was psychological.

Names were removed.

A name anchors a man to lineage, memory, responsibility, and place. It situates him inside a story that existed before capture. Stripping a man of his name severed him from that story. Renaming was not administrative.

It was deliberate erasure.

You are no longer who you were.
You are what you are told.

A man without a name is easier to command.
A man without history is easier to redefine.
A man without lineage is easier to isolate.

This was not symbolic. It was functional.

Control Had to Be Constant

For those born into slavery, the breaking was not a single event.

It had to be reinforced.

Every day carried reminders:

- You will never own land

- You will never control your labor

- You will never protect your family

- You will never decide your future

Skill did not equal authority.
Strength did not equal respect.

Black men could be trusted with tools, animals, machinery, and responsibility—but never with control. That boundary was absolute. The purpose was not to prevent work.

It was to prevent ownership of outcome.

A man who controls the outcome controls himself. That could not be allowed.

Brutality as Instruction

Whippings, mutilations, public hangings, sexual humiliation, and psychological torture were not random acts of cruelty.

They were lessons.

They taught where the line was.
They taught who held power.
They taught what resistance would cost.

Violence was staged. It was witnessed. It was remembered. It did not need to be constant—but it had to be visible, renewable, and unforgettable.

Control decays if it is not refreshed.

The Policing of Control

Slave patrols extended this system beyond the plantation. Their purpose was not moral enforcement. It was containment.

Runaways threatened the system before they threatened profit. A man who escaped proved that control was not total—and that possibility was more dangerous than lost labor.

Brutality followed Black men into forests, roads, and neighboring territories. The right to move became criminal. The desire for freedom became punishable.

Violence became policy.

The Targeting of Manhood

This violence was not gender-neutral.

Black men were targeted because manhood itself represented danger. A man who believed he could protect, lead, intervene, or define himself threatened the system's authority at its root.

So, masculinity was punished.
Leadership was destroyed.
Intervention was criminalized.

Teaching the sons

The system understood that men teach their sons.

So Black men were not only controlled as individuals—they were restricted as teachers. Pride was beaten out. Resistance was punished. Authority was mocked, then removed.

Only one lesson was allowed to survive:

Nothing matters but the work.

This ensured continuity.

Why Economics Comes After

Only after this conditioning could large-scale labor function.

Economics was not the beginning of slavery.
It was the benefit of control already established.

This is why brutality intensified whenever Black men approached autonomy.
This is why it persisted long after slavery ended.

Because the true objective was never just labor.

It was control.

By the time slavery formally ended, the work of breaking Black men was already advanced.

The body had been conditioned.
The mind had been fragmented.
Leadership had been punished.
Identity had been destabilized.

But what came next would prove something even more important:

Violence was never the only tool.
Law would finish what brutality started.

When the Civil War ended in 1865, America declared slavery abolished. But the declaration came with a condition so precise, so intentional, that it would shape Black male existence for the next century and beyond.

The 13th Amendment did not eliminate slavery outright.
It redefined it.

Slavery was abolished *except as punishment for a crime.*

That single clause was not incidental language. It was a structural escape hatch—one that allowed the state to legally return Black men to conditions indistinguishable from slavery, so long as arrest and conviction could be secured.

Freedom, on paper, now depended on behavior.
And behavior would be policed.

This is where the system evolved.

Chains were replaced with charges.
Plantations were replaced with prisons.
Overseers were replaced with sheriffs, judges, and wardens.

Black men were no longer owned by individuals.
They were owned by law.

What followed was not a failure of Reconstruction.
It was a reaction to it.

For the first time, Black men existed without chains and with memory intact. They remembered structure. They remembered leadership. They remembered responsibility. And when given even limited access, they began to rebuild.

That rebuilding terrified the same power structure that had once relied on brute force.

So, the system did what it had always done when Black men approached autonomy.

It changed the rules.

CHAPTER 5

Breaking the Black Male Mind

You can shackle a body
and still lose control of a man.

So, the system went deeper.

Once Black men were reduced to labor units, the next phase was
not physical—it was psychological. The architects of slavery
understood something modern audiences struggle to accept:
lasting control requires reshaping how a man understands
himself.

This was not accidental trauma.
It was engineered.

What happened to Black men in America was not random
cruelty. It was calculated behavioral conditioning. Systems that
last for centuries are never built on impulse. They are built on
observation, trial, error, and refinement.

Plantation records, overseer manuals, colonial correspondence,
and economic logs all reveal the same priority: controlling the
mind mattered more than controlling the body.

Force could make a man work.
Fear could make a man comply.

But psychological fracture could make a man police himself.

That was the true goal.

Breaking Comes Before Obedience

Violence was rarely private.
This was intentional.

Whippings, beatings, brandings, mutilations, and executions
were often staged in front of other enslaved people. The real
target was not only the man being punished. The real target was
everyone watching.

The system understood what modern psychology now calls
vicarious conditioning.

People do not learn only from what happens to them.
They learn by watching what happens to others.

A Black man watching another man punished learned where the
invisible line was. He learned what confidence cost. He learned
that standing tall invited attention—and attention invited pain.

This trained fear into the nervous system of the community itself.

The overseer did not need to be everywhere.
Fear did the work for him.

Over time, repeated exposure to unpredictable violence reshapes
behavior at a biological level. Modern trauma research shows
that chronic threat alters how the brain processes fear, memory,
impulse control, and emotional regulation.

This produces hypervigilance.

Hypervigilance is not a defect.
It is a survival adaptation.

But when it is inherited across generations, it begins to look like culture to the outside world—when in truth it is trauma responding to danger that never fully left.

Unpredictability as Weapon

Stability is the foundation of mental health.
So stability had to be destroyed.

A Black man never knew when he would be sold, punished, separated, or killed. Cause and effect were deliberately blurred. Obedience did not guarantee safety. Compliance did not guarantee survival.

When punishment is unpredictable, the mind shifts into survival mode.

In survival mode:

- Long-term planning becomes dangerous

- Trust becomes risky

- Attachment becomes liability

A man narrows his focus to the present moment because anything beyond it can be taken without warning.

This is how hope is quietly strangled.

This psychological condition would later be named *learned helplessness*—a phenomenon formally studied in the 20th century, but practiced long before it had language.

When a person experiences repeated punishment that appears unavoidable, they may stop attempting resistance altogether— even when resistance later becomes possible.

This was not weakness.
It was conditioning.

Identity Stripping

African societies tied manhood to dignity, role, belonging, and responsibility. Enslavement attacked all four simultaneously.

Names were stripped.
Titles were erased.
Family authority was removed.
Men were forbidden from leading their own households.

In psychological terms, this is called *identity stripping*.

Identity stripping disorients a person by removing social role, name, authority, and relational power at the same time. A man who does not know where he stands cannot organize others. A man without an internal compass cannot lead.

This was not just abuse.
This was identity warfare.

A man without identity is easier to redefine.
A man without definition is easier to control.

Division as Design

The system also engineered internal fracture.

Some enslaved men were given symbolic authority over others—
not real power, but enough to create resentment, distrust, and
competition. This trained men to watch each other. To report on
each other. To survive at the expense of unity.

Divide strength.
Diffuse loyalty.
Install fear of brothers.

This pattern did not end on plantations.

It later reappeared in prisons, housing projects, and communities
shaped by enforced scarcity. Division was not natural. It was
taught as survival.

Black men did not become fractured because they were flawed.
They became fractured because unity was punished.

Shame, Humiliation, and Masculinity

Public punishment did more than enforce obedience.
It eroded dignity.

Repeated exposure to humiliation creates internalized powerlessness. Over time, powerlessness is mistaken for weakness—by others, and eventually by the man himself.

This is where shame takes root.

Strength became dangerous.
Leadership became lethal.
Intelligence became something to hide.
Silence became survival.

These adaptations were rational responses to irrational conditions.

But survival strategies become liabilities when carried into environments that require connection, planning, and emotional presence.

Sexual Mythology and Surveillance

Black men were simultaneously dehumanized and hypersexualized. They were depicted as animalistic, dangerous, incapable of restraint.

This contradiction served a purpose.

If a man is viewed as dangerous by default, then controlling him becomes morally acceptable. Surveillance becomes protection. Violence becomes order.

That framing still echoes today.

The Long Tail of Trauma

Suppressed identity does not disappear.
It mutates.

Modern science now recognizes that trauma can be transmitted across generations—not genetically, but behaviorally. Through stress response. Through emotional modeling. Through what fathers are allowed to show and what they are punished for expressing.

Sons learn how to feel by watching men who were trained to suppress.

This is not destiny.
This is learned survival.

The modern world looks at Black men and sees guarded emotion, anger, distance, hyper-independence, mistrust.

What it does not see is the system that trained those behaviors as necessary.

What it does not see is that none of this was random.

Naming the Injury

Breaking the Black male mind was never about destroying intelligence. It was about severing alignment—between effort

44

and reward, between strength and safety, between identity and agency.

Fragmentation followed.

Fragmentation looks like volatility.
It looks like inconsistency.
It looks like absence.

But it is not chaos.

It is residue.

You cannot heal what you refuse to name.

And until this psychological history is acknowledged honestly, Black men will continue to be judged by symptoms while the cause remains untouched.

The breaking was not accidental.
It was not chaotic.
It was not cultural.

It was engineered.

And engineered systems leave predictable scars.

Not because Black men are flawed.
But because Black men were targeted.

Where This Leads Next

Once the mind was fractured, control no longer required constant violence.

Policy could finish the work.

And that is where the story goes next.

CHAPTER 6

The Erasure of Black Fatherhood

The destruction of Black fatherhood was not a side effect of history.

It was a strategy.

If you want to destabilize a people across generations, you do not start with the children. Children adapt. Children survive. Children can be shaped later.

You start with the men who would teach them how to stand.

From the earliest days of enslavement, Black fathers were treated as expendable—not because they were unnecessary, but because they were powerful. A father represents continuity. He carries memory forward. He models authority, protection, discipline, and responsibility in real time.

A present father interrupts domination.

So, he had to be removed—physically first, then psychologically, then institutionally.

On plantations, Black men were routinely separated from their partners and children. Families were not considered units; they were inventories. A man could be sold away at any moment, regardless of his role in his children's lives, regardless of attachment, regardless of obligation.

Love was treated as weakness.
Attachment was punished.

This was not random cruelty.

It was policy.

A father who could not protect his children was forced to watch his authority dissolve in front of them. A boy who watched his father rendered powerless learned a dangerous lesson early: masculinity does not guarantee safety. Protection does not guarantee preservation.

That lesson embeds itself deep.

Black men were denied the ability to fulfill the most basic responsibilities associated with manhood—providing, protecting, guiding—and were later blamed for failing to meet those responsibilities.

This contradiction did not end with slavery.

It evolved.

After emancipation, the system shifted from overt separation to structural removal. Black men were pushed into labor arrangements that required constant movement. Sharecropping contracts trapped men in cycles of debt that made stability nearly impossible.

Vagrancy laws criminalized unemployment, allowing Black men to be arrested simply for existing without sanctioned work.

A man could be jailed for not working—
yet denied access to work that paid a living wage.

This is how fatherhood becomes fragile.

A man cannot remain present in his home if survival requires constant displacement. He cannot plan for his family if tomorrow is legally uncertain. Over time, presence becomes intermittent. Authority becomes symbolic. Responsibility becomes theoretical.

The absence was not chosen.

It was engineered.

As policies hardened, the narrative shifted.

The system began to speak *about* Black fathers instead of acknowledging what it had done to remove them. Absence was reframed as apathy. Structural barriers were reframed as moral failure. Black men were portrayed as irresponsible, unreliable, and disinterested in family life.

This lie stuck—because it was repeated without context.

What was never acknowledged is that no group of men in history has been systematically denied the ability to function as fathers and then judged for failing to do so.

You cannot legislate a man out of his home and then shame him for not being there.

This erasure had compounding effects.

Without consistent father presence, boys grew up without real-time modeling of manhood. Masculinity was learned indirectly—through peers, media, authority figures who punished rather than taught, and environments that rewarded toughness over clarity.

Authority became something imposed, not demonstrated. Discipline became punishment, not instruction.

Girls grew up associating male presence with instability or impermanence. Trust became conditional. Expectations were lowered for men, even as resentment quietly grew.

And women—forced into roles they were never meant to carry alone—became nurturers and enforcers, providers and protectors. They did the best they could with what they were given.

But no amount of strength can replace what was intentionally removed.

This is where clarity matters.

Acknowledging the erasure of Black fatherhood is not an indictment of Black women. It is an indictment of systems that made male presence illegal, impractical, or unsustainable.

Women adapted.
Children adapted.
Men adapted.

But adaptation is not healing.

The absence of fathers created a generational knowledge gap. Boys were not taught how to regulate emotion, navigate authority, or carry responsibility in healthy ways. Girls were not shown consistent male protection and leadership.

What followed was not chaos.

It was improvisation.

And improvisation under trauma produces uneven results.

This chapter is not about longing for a fantasy of the past. It is about naming a fracture that still shapes relationships, expectations, and self-perception today.

Black fatherhood was not lost.

It was removed.

And until that removal is acknowledged honestly, conversations about responsibility will continue to start in the wrong place.

CHAPTER 7

Jim Crow: Fear as Law

When slavery ended, control did not.

It changed uniforms.

The chains were removed from the wrists, but they reappeared in the law. Where plantations enforced obedience through violence alone, Jim Crow perfected something more efficient: fear backed by legality.

For Black men, Jim Crow was not merely a set of social customs.

It was a governing philosophy.

It was designed to remind them—daily—that freedom had limits, and those limits were enforced with terror.

The message was consistent and unmistakable:

You are free to exist,
but not to rise.

Black men were told where they could live, where they could work, where they could walk, where they could sit, and where they could look. Every boundary was reinforced not only by statute, but by the threat of violence—often public, often celebrated, and almost always unpunished.

Lynching was not random brutality.

It was social regulation.

A Black man did not have to commit a crime to be killed. He only had to be perceived as confident, successful, educated, organized, or insufficiently deferential.

Fear was the point.
The spectacle was the lesson.

Men learned quickly that visibility was dangerous.

A man who spoke too loudly risked his life.
A man who earned too much risked suspicion.
A man who protected his dignity risked retaliation.

So, survival required performance.

Black men learned how to make themselves small. How to avoid eye contact. How to lower their voices. How to laugh off insults. How to endure humiliation without response.

This was not cowardice.

It was calculus.

A man who wanted to see his children grow up learned when to disappear.

Jim Crow laws did more than restrict movement.

They criminalized aspiration.

Economic success was framed as theft.
Education was framed as threat.
Organization was framed as insurrection.

A Black man who attempted to vote was beaten or killed.
A Black man who attempted to own land was displaced.
A Black man who attempted to organize labor was crushed.

This is where the contradiction deepened.

Black men were told to be providers—while being denied stable work.
Told to be leaders—while being punished for influence.
Told to be citizens—while being excluded from civic life.

The result was not passivity.

It was fragmentation.

Some men retreated inward, prioritizing survival over visibility.
Others pushed back, absorbed the risks, and paid the price.
Families learned to negotiate fear together, teaching children
what not to do rather than what they could become.

Fear became inheritance.

Jim Crow also redefined masculinity through humiliation. A
man's inability to protect his family from racial terror was used
to emasculate him psychologically. The system did not need to
defeat Black men physically if it could convince them that
resistance was futile.

This is how masculinity becomes distorted.

Strength is redirected inward as anger or outward as recklessness.
Silence becomes wisdom.
Distance becomes safety.
Vulnerability becomes dangerous.

Then the system points to these adaptations as evidence of defect.

But Jim Crow was not designed to produce healthy men.

It was designed to produce compliant ones.

Even so, Black men did not stop resisting.

They built churches, schools, businesses, and mutual aid societies. They organized quietly when loud organization meant death. They protected each other when the law refused to.

But every act of self-sufficiency was met with retaliation.

The lesson was reinforced again and again:

Stability invites scrutiny.
Success invites punishment.

This is how a people are trained to associate advancement with danger.

Jim Crow did not merely restrict rights.

It conditioned nervous systems.

It taught Black men how to read rooms for threats. How to suppress impulse. How to survive under constant surveillance.

Those lessons did not vanish when Jim Crow laws were repealed. They were carried forward—into workplaces, schools, relationships, and parenting.

Before mass incarceration,
before modern policing,
before the War on Drugs,

there was Jim Crow—teaching Black men how to endure without ever feeling safe.

That fear would later be repackaged as criminality.
That vigilance would later be labeled aggression.
That restraint would later be misread as absence.

But it began as law.

And fear, once legalized, does not disappear quietly.

CHAPTER 8

Voting Rights and Power Removal

Power does not disappear on its own.
It is taken—or redirected.

After slavery and during Jim Crow, Black men understood
something intuitively: without political power, every other
freedom was temporary. Land could be seized. Businesses could
be burned. Families could be terrorized. But the ability to
influence law threatened the entire structure of control.

So, it had to be neutralized.

On paper, Black men were granted the right to vote. In practice,
that right was surrounded by traps—poll taxes, literacy tests,
arbitrary "understanding clauses," and grandfather clauses
designed to exclude Black men while preserving white access.

Voting was transformed from a right into a risk.

A Black man who attempted to register could lose his job, his
home, or his life. Employers monitored voter rolls. Landowners
retaliated. Sheriffs enforced "order" with clubs and bullets.

The message was unmistakable: participation would be punished.

This is how political power is removed without formally
revoking it.

Black men were not simply barred from the ballot. They were terrorized away from it. Fear became the deterrent. The cost of participation was made so high that abstention became the safer option.

The removal of political power had cascading effects.

Without voting power, Black men could not protect their communities through policy. They could not influence policing, education, housing, or labor laws. They could not elect officials who reflected their interests or experiences. Decisions about Black life was made without Black input.

This was not abstraction.
It was consequence.

When laws are written by those who do not experience their impact, harm becomes inevitable. When enforcement is controlled by those insulated from accountability, abuse becomes routine.

Black men learned this early.

Political engagement did not lead to protection—it led to exposure. Organizing drew attention. Attention invited retaliation. Silence, once again, became survival.

But silence comes at a cost.

A man who cannot influence the rules that govern his life is reduced to reacting to them. Over time, this erodes investment. Why commit to systems that offer no voice and no return?

This is how disengagement is manufactured.

Later generations would be criticized for low voter turnout, civic apathy, or mistrust in government. Rarely was the historical conditioning acknowledged. You cannot terrorize a people away from political participation for a century and then shame them for distrusting the process.

The removal of voting power also severed a critical feedback loop. Elected officials had no incentive to serve Black communities because Black men could not reliably hold them accountable at the polls.

Neglect became policy.
Powerlessness became routine.

Even when legal barriers fell, the psychological ones remained. Fear does not evaporate when laws change. Memory lingers. Stories are passed down. Children learn what their fathers learned: visibility can be dangerous.

This is how political trauma becomes generational.

Black men did not stop caring about their communities. They stopped trusting the systems that governed them. They built parallel structures—churches, mutual aid networks, informal economies—outside the reach of the ballot box.

These adaptations were rational responses to exclusion.

But they also reinforced the system's narrative: that Black men were disengaged, irresponsible, or uninterested in civic life.

Again, the cause was erased.
The effect was pathologized.

The removal of voting rights was not just about ballots. It was about severing Black men from formal power while holding them responsible for outcomes they could not influence.

That contradiction would define every phase that followed.

A man without political power can be controlled through economics.
A man without economic power can be controlled through law enforcement.
A man without legal protection can be controlled through fear.

Voting rights were the keystone.

Once removed, the entire structure of exclusion could be built on top.

CHAPTER 9

Redlining and Economic Containment

If slavery controlled the body and Jim Crow controlled behavior, redlining controlled possibility.

Economic power does not require chains or terror to be effective. It only requires boundaries—quiet ones. Invisible ones. Lines drawn not on the ground, but on maps, loan applications, and access itself.

Redlining was not accidental discrimination.
It was deliberate containment.

Through federal housing policies, banking practices, and real estate covenants, Black communities were boxed into specific neighborhoods and denied access to credit, investment, and appreciation. These areas were marked—often literally outlined in red—as "high risk," regardless of the character or income of the people who lived there.

A Black man could work every day of his life and still be denied the single most reliable path to generational stability in America: home ownership.

This mattered because wealth in America has rarely been built through wages alone. It has been built through assets—land, property, and equity passed down across generations.

Redlining ensured that Black men were locked out of that process while still being taxed, policed, and blamed as if they were fully included.

The contradiction deepened.

Black men were expected to provide stability for their families while being denied access to stable neighborhoods. They were told to invest in their communities while those same communities were starved of resources.

Schools were underfunded.
Infrastructure deteriorated.
Businesses struggled to access capital.

When neighborhoods suffered, the blame was placed on the residents—not the policies that engineered decline.

This is how containment masquerades as choice.

A man does not choose poverty when the exits are blocked.
He adapts to it.

Redlining also intensified surveillance. Contained communities are easier to monitor, easier to police, and easier to criminalize. Overcrowding created tension. Limited opportunity created competition. Stress became ambient.

And when problems emerged—as they always do under pressure—they were framed as cultural failures rather than predictable outcomes of enforced scarcity.

Black men living in redlined neighborhoods were seen as suspect by default. Their presence outside those neighborhoods invited scrutiny. Their attempts to move into white neighborhoods were met with hostility, violence, or legal obstruction.

Economic mobility became dangerous.

This is where the narrative about "bad neighborhoods" was born—not because the people were inherently bad, but because investment was intentionally withheld.

When decay followed, it was cited as justification for further neglect.

A closed loop.

Redlining also shaped how Black men related to work. Long commutes. Limited job access. Wage stagnation. Men were forced to expend more energy for less return.

Exhaustion became normal.
Planning became difficult.
Frustration hardened.

A man who works tirelessly and still cannot improve his circumstances begins to question the value of compliance. This is not laziness. It is pattern recognition.

The system tightened the narrative.

Economic struggle was reframed as irresponsibility.
Over-policing was framed as crime prevention.
Disinvestment was framed as market logic.

At every stage, cause was obscured and effect was amplified.

Redlining did not just limit where Black men could live. It limited where they could dream. It constrained imagination. It trained men to think in terms of survival instead of expansion.

And yet, even within these boundaries, Black men built what they could.

Informal economies emerged.
Mutual aid networks strengthened.
Hustle became ingenuity under constraint.

Those adaptations would later be criminalized.

But here—at this stage—they were responses to containment.

Redlining ensured that when America spoke about opportunity, it spoke in a language Black men were not allowed to learn. Inequality persisted without overt violence—enforced through paperwork instead of whips.

And when the consequences surfaced, the system pointed to the men trapped inside it and asked why they had not escaped.

Economic containment is most effective when it convinces its victims the walls are natural.

They were not.

They were drawn.

CHAPTER 10

The GI Bill and Stolen Opportunity

Opportunity is not just about access.
It is about timing.

When the Servicemen's Readjustment Act of 1944—commonly known as the GI Bill—was introduced after World War II, it was framed as a reward for service. It promised returning veterans access to education, low-interest home loans, business financing, and job training. On its face, the legislation appeared race-neutral.

In practice, it became one of the most effective tools for widening the racial wealth gap in American history.

Black men fought for this country.
They bled for it.
Many died for it.

Yet when they returned home, the benefits promised to them were filtered through local and state institutions that were already hostile to their advancement.

The federal government did not administer the GI Bill directly. It delegated implementation to local banks, university admissions offices, housing authorities, and employment boards—many of which operated openly under Jim Crow norms.

As a result:

Banks denied mortgage and business loans to Black veterans, citing "risk" while approving white applicants with similar or weaker financial profiles.

Universities—especially predominantly white institutions—restricted or outright refused Black enrollment, funneling applicants toward underfunded historically Black colleges that lacked capacity for the surge.

Trade unions blocked Black veterans from apprenticeship programs that served as gateways to stable, middle-class employment.

Real estate boards enforced racially restrictive covenants that barred Black families from purchasing homes in newly developing suburbs.

The GI Bill did not fail Black men by accident.
It was administered through systems that had already decided where Black men belonged—and where they did not.

White veterans were ushered into colleges, suburban neighborhoods, and long-term careers. They accumulated degrees, property, and professional networks that compounded across generations.

Their children inherited stability.
Their grandchildren inherited wealth.

Black veterans, by contrast, were often shut out.

A Black man could qualify on paper and still be denied in practice. He could apply for a Veterans Administration–backed mortgage and be told no eligible homes were available in areas where his family was permitted to live. He could seek higher education and be redirected to overcrowded institutions with limited funding, limited alumni networks, and limited post-graduation mobility. He could attempt to use job placement benefits only to discover that access was controlled by unions and employers who excluded him by design.

This was not simply denial.
It was theft.

The GI Bill represented one of the largest wealth-building initiatives in American history. By some estimates, it helped create the modern white middle class. Black men were excluded from that transfer while still being expected to compete in the economy it produced.

This exclusion compounded every prior injustice.

Men who had survived the aftermath of slavery, Jim Crow terror, voter suppression, and economic containment now watched white peers—many less experienced, many less credentialed— leapfrog into prosperity.

Resentment was not irrational.
It was earned.

And still, Black men were told to be patient.
To work harder.
To wait their turn.

A turn that never came.

The psychological impact was profound. The GI Bill became a visible, measurable example of opportunity being deliberately withheld. It confirmed a truth, Black men already suspected:

Effort did not guarantee reward in America.
Loyalty did not guarantee inclusion.
Service did not guarantee respect.

This realization reshaped how Black men approached institutions. Trust eroded. Cynicism grew. Commitment weakened.

Why invest fully in a system that repeatedly demonstrates its willingness to exclude you?

The exclusion also produced generational consequences.

White families used GI benefits to purchase homes in suburban developments whose value appreciated dramatically over time. Those homes were passed down, leveraged for business capital, or used to finance higher education for the next generation.

Black families, locked out, remained renters in redlined neighborhoods where property values stagnated or declined, schools remained underfunded, and policing intensified.

The gap widened—not because Black men did not serve, but because their service was not rewarded equally.

This is where the myth of "equal opportunity" collapses under scrutiny.

Opportunity was distributed selectively.

And when Black men failed to advance at the same rate, stagnation was reframed as personal failure instead of structural exclusion.

The GI Bill did not just create winners and losers.
It created narratives—about who deserved success and who did not.

Those narratives persist.

They echo every time Black men are told hard work alone is enough.
Every time history is ignored.
Every time exclusion is rewritten as deficiency.

The stolen opportunity of the GI Bill was not an isolated injustice. It reinforced a recurring pattern: advancement offered to some, denied to others, then used as evidence of inherent difference.

For Black men, this moment clarified the direction of the country.

America would benefit from their labor, their service, and their sacrifice—
but not from their prosperity.

And that truth would shape every economic decision that followed.

CHAPTER 11

COINTELPRO and the War on Black Leadership

When exclusion was no longer enough, suppression became necessary.

By the mid-20th century, Black men were no longer only surviving within constraints. They were organizing, educating, and building parallel institutions that directly addressed gaps created by segregation and state neglect—schools, free breakfast programs, health clinics, tenant unions, political education classes, and armed community patrols.

This shift triggered federal response.

The U.S. government did not misunderstand Black leadership. It identified it as a strategic threat. Internal FBI memoranda from the 1950s and 1960s explicitly described Black nationalist organizations as dangers to "internal security," regardless of whether they advocated violence.

COINTELPRO—short for Counter Intelligence Program—was initiated in 1956 under FBI Director J. Edgar Hoover. While originally aimed at the Communist Party USA, it was expanded throughout the 1960s to target civil rights groups, Black nationalist organizations, and anti-war movements.

Among its primary targets were Black men.

Not criminal organizations.
Not gangs.
But leaders.

Men who organized communities.
Men who articulated systemic critique.
Men who created self-sustaining alternatives to state dependency.

FBI documents declassified in the 1970s confirm that COINTELPRO's stated goal was to "prevent the rise of a Black messiah" who could unify and mobilize Black communities politically and economically.

The government understood that disciplined, educated, community-oriented Black masculinity undermined centuries of control.

So, suppression moved underground.

COINTELPRO relied heavily on psychological warfare, not just arrests. Surveillance was constant. Telephones were tapped without warrants. Mail was intercepted. Meetings were infiltrated by informants. Forged letters were sent to create suspicion, infighting, and paranoia.

Most critically, Black men were used against Black men.

Informants were recruited through coercion, blackmail, financial incentives, or threat of prosecution. In many cases, individuals were pressured into cooperation under the threat of long prison sentences.

Trust became a weapon.

Brotherhood was deliberately poisoned.

Organizations were destabilized from the inside, ensuring collapse without the need for public trials or visible repression.

Addiction was also leveraged.

Heroin and other narcotics flooded Black neighborhoods during this same period, coinciding with the dismantling of Black political organizations. While drug proliferation is often discussed abstractly, multiple congressional inquiries—including the 1975 Church Committee—documented intelligence-agency awareness of narcotics trafficking intersecting with political destabilization.

Addiction eroded discipline.
Compromised leadership.
Fragmented households.

A sober, organized man posed a threat to authority.
A distracted; addicted man was easier to manage.

Groups such as the Black Panther Party were targeted not because they promoted violence, but because they demonstrated structure. Their community programs fed children, provided medical screenings, monitored police behavior, and educated citizens on constitutional rights.

That example could not be allowed to spread.

Leaders were publicly discredited through media leaks.
Internal disputes were provoked through falsified
correspondence.
Arrests were staged on minor or fabricated charges.
Assassinations were carried out under the cover of law
enforcement action.

The 1969 killing of Fred Hampton in Chicago—later ruled a
coordinated state operation—became a clear message.

Organize, and you will be eliminated.
Trust, and it will be exploited.

The effects of COINTELPRO extended far beyond the
organizations it destroyed.

It taught Black men that leadership invited surveillance.
That visibility invited death.
That unity carried lethal consequences.

Withdrawal became survival.

Ironically, once leadership was dismantled, the same institutions
blamed Black communities for lacking leadership, discipline,
and cohesion.

The arsonist became the critic.

Although COINTELPRO was officially terminated in 1971, its
tactics did not disappear. Surveillance, infiltration, and the
criminalization of Black political organization continued under
new frameworks—drug enforcement, gang databases, domestic
terrorism labels, and expanded policing powers.

What had once been overt counterintelligence became administrative control.

Black men learned a lasting lesson:

Progress without permission would be punished.
Reform would be slow and conditional.
Independence would not be tolerated.

This realization pushed many men back into survival mode.

If organizing leads to death,
and compliance leads to stagnation,
the remaining space narrows.

The war on Black leadership cleared the ground for what followed.

Once leaders were removed and trust was broken, policies could devastate communities without coordinated resistance.

COINTELPRO did not merely silence voices.

It prepared the conditions.

And what followed would no longer target leadership alone.

It would target survival itself.

CHAPTER 12

Welfare and the Removal of the Black Father

After leadership was dismantled, the next target was structure.

If COINTELPRO neutralized organized Black masculinity from the outside, welfare policy undermined it from the inside—quietly, administratively, and with plausible deniability.

This phase did not arrive wearing the face of hatred.
It arrived wearing the language of help.

Public assistance programs expanded during the mid-20th century in response to real poverty, real displacement, and real deprivation. Black communities had been systematically excluded from wealth creation, home ownership, and stable employment. Assistance, on its surface, was necessary.

But the design of that assistance mattered.

Under many welfare policies—particularly Aid to Families with Dependent Children (AFDC)—benefits were conditioned on household composition. A man's presence in the home could reduce or eliminate eligibility. Caseworkers were authorized to conduct unannounced inspections, often referred to as "man-in-the-house" rules.

Inspectors searched for evidence of male presence:
extra shoes,
men's clothing,
a toothbrush,
a jacket,
signs that a father lived there.

If found, assistance could be cut.

The message was not ambiguous.

A Black man in the home was treated as a financial liability.

This did not remove fathers with whips or chains.
It removed them with incentives.

Men were forced into impossible choices: remain present and risk losing food, housing, and medical support for their children—or step away so those resources could remain intact. Presence became sacrifice. Absence became survival.

Over time, absence normalized.

This was not the result of individual failure.
It was policy design.

A system that ties family survival to the removal of male authority is not neutral. It reshapes behavior predictably. It conditions outcomes. It engineers' absence while claiming benevolence.

Women were positioned as the sole recognized heads of household. Men were rendered unofficial—present in reality, absent on paper. Authority shifted from family structure to bureaucracy.

The provider role was replaced with a check.
Leadership was replaced with compliance.
Accountability moved from relationship to regulation.

And once again, adaptation was mislabeled.

Men who stepped away were labeled irresponsible.
Men who resisted were labeled controlling.
Men who questioned the system were labeled unstable.

The structure itself remained unquestioned.

This policy-driven removal compounded earlier damage. Black men already denied stable employment, fair wages, union access, housing equity, and political power were now told their presence harmed the very families they were expected to lead.

What does a man become when his existence is framed as a problem?

Some internalized the message and disengaged completely.
Others hovered at the margins—emotionally present but structurally excluded.
Others rejected the system entirely.

None of these outcomes produced stability.
All of them produced blame.

As fatherhood eroded, the narrative hardened. Black women were praised for resilience and strength—rightfully—while Black men were condemned for absence, without acknowledging the policies that engineered that absence as rational behavior.

This framing sowed gender fracture.

Women were forced into roles of sole provider, disciplinarian, protector, and stabilizer. Men were stripped of authority and opportunity, then judged for failing to perform roles they were actively discouraged from occupying.

This was not empowerment.
It was displacement.

And displacement breeds resentment.

The removal of Black fathers through welfare policy did not occur in isolation. It followed decades of economic containment, political disenfranchisement, leadership suppression, and labor exclusion.

Once men were pushed out of the home, the intergenerational transfer of manhood became even more fragile. Boys grew up without daily male modeling—not because fathers did not care, but because presence was penalized.

This would later be reframed as cultural dysfunction.

But it began as policy.

Welfare did not destroy Black families on its own.
It exploited fractures already created—and deepened them.

And once this phase was complete, the system no longer needed to disguise its intent.

Compassion would recede.
Punishment would replace it.

CHAPTER 13

The Lockout

Once the father was removed from the home, the final door could be shut.

The Lockout was not a single law or policy.
It was a condition—engineered through the convergence of economics, legislation, and enforcement.

By this stage, Black men were no longer merely excluded from opportunity. They were systematically prevented from reentering it once displaced.

Survival stopped being difficult.
It became criminal.

Employment pathways narrowed rapidly in the late 20th century. Manufacturing jobs—once a primary source of stable income for working-class Black men—were outsourced, automated, or eliminated. Union access declined. Hiring discrimination persisted behind neutral language, credential requirements, and subjective evaluations.

A Black man could apply endlessly and still be told he "Wasn't a good fit."

At the same time, penalties hardened.

Minor charges became permanent records.
Arrests—often without conviction—followed men indefinitely.
Background checks became filters.

Professional licenses were denied.
Applications quietly disappeared.

A felony was no longer a sentence.
It was exile.

Housing access was restricted.
Loans were denied.
Student aid was revoked.
Voting rights were stripped.
Firearm ownership—self-defense—became illegal.

Every formal path back to legitimacy was obstructed.

This is where intent revealed itself.

Punishment was no longer about correction.
It was about removal.

And yet expectations remained.

Black men were still expected to provide.
Still expected to support families.
Still expected to contribute to communities.

But the legal avenues to do so had been sealed.

This contradiction is where desperation takes shape.

A man without access to legal work does not stop needing
money. His children do not stop needing food. Survival does not
pause because permission has been revoked.

The Lockout did not eliminate need.
It eliminated permission.

This is where informal economies grew—not as rebellion, but as response.

Underground markets did not emerge because Black men rejected legitimacy. They emerged because legitimacy rejected Black men. When formal systems deny access, parallel systems form. This is not unique to Black communities. It is a predictable response to exclusion.

The system watched carefully.

It studied routes.
Documented behaviors.
Tracked survival patterns.

Instead of reopening doors, it prepared consequences.

Law enforcement strategies adapted to target these informal economies. Sentencing laws escalated. Surveillance expanded. Penalties multiplied. What had begun as exclusion now became justification.

This is the moment most misunderstood in public discourse.

The rise of underground economies is treated as evidence of criminal nature rather than proof of systematic exclusion. Cause is ignored. Effect is punished.

People do not abandon legitimacy unless legitimacy abandons them first.

The Lockout also intensified internal fracture.

Scarcity narrowed trust.
Competition replaced collaboration.
Cooperation became risky.

This is how survival rewires morality.

Adaptation was once again mislabeled as defect.

The Lockout was effective because it did not require hatred. It operated through paperwork, policy, and procedure while claiming neutrality.

A door closed quietly is still a door closed.

The Lockout did not create criminals.
It created corners.

And in corners, men do what they must to survive.

The system understood this.

That understanding would soon be weaponized.

CHAPTER 14

The Hustle-Syndrome

The Hustle-Syndrome did not emerge from ambition.
It emerged from exclusion.

When legitimate pathways were sealed, Black men were forced to redefine survival. Hustle was not a lifestyle choice. It was a compensatory behavior—an adaptive response to a system that removed permission while maintaining expectation.

The message was clear but unspoken:

Provide—without access.
Succeed—without infrastructure.
Compete—without protection.

Hustle became the substitute.

At its core, the Hustle-Syndrome is not about illegal activity. It is about improvisation under constraint. When stability is structurally denied, flexibility becomes currency. When long-term planning is repeatedly invalidated, short-term opportunity becomes rational.

This is not pathology.
It is pattern recognition.

Black men learned that formal systems did not reward patience, loyalty, or compliance. They rewarded proximity, access, and sponsorship—resources consistently withheld. So, value had to be created outside sanctioned channels.

Hustle filled the gap.

Multiple income streams replaced single careers because careers were unreliable. Side work replaced stability because stability was conditional. Speed replaced patience because waiting had historically led nowhere.

This rewired priorities.

Long-term investment felt unrealistic.
Delayed gratification felt unsafe.
Consistency felt fragile.

In that environment, adaptability became more valuable than credentials.

The Hustle-Syndrome also reshaped identity.

A man's worth became tied to output, not alignment. Movement replaced direction. Being busy replaced being stable. Visibility replaced sustainability.

If a man slowed down, he risked falling behind permanently.

Rest became guilt.
Stillness became threat.
Reflection became luxury.

This is how burnout becomes normalized.

The system then criminalized the very adaptations it forced. Informal work was labeled fraud. Side income was labeled evasion. Street-level commerce was labeled predation—without acknowledging why formal access was absent.

Once again, cause was erased.
Effect was punished.

The Hustle-Syndrome also fractured trust.

When opportunity is scarce, collaboration feels dangerous.
Sharing information risks losing advantage. Loyalty becomes
transactional. Brotherhood weakens under pressure.

This is not moral failure.
It is scarcity psychology.

The syndrome trained men to rely on themselves because
reliance on institutions had proven unreliable. But self-reliance
without support turns inward. It isolates. It exhausts.

A man can hustle himself into collapse.

Culturally, hustle was later glamorized—reframed as grit, grind,
and ambition. But this reframing obscured the origin. Hustle was
celebrated without questioning why it was necessary in the first
place.

Grinding became virtue.
Exhaustion became badge.
Struggle became identity.

Meanwhile, the absence of safety nets remained unaddressed.

The Hustle-Syndrome also interfered with family life.
Inconsistent schedules disrupted presence. Stress narrowed
emotional bandwidth. Risk-taking followed men home.

Children learned that survival required constant motion.
That rest was irresponsible.
That security was temporary.

These lessons passed quietly across generations.

Importantly, the Hustle-Syndrome did not produce wealth at scale. It produced movement without accumulation. Energy was expended without compounding return. While others-built equity through assets and institutions, Black men were forced into cycles that reset repeatedly.

Hustle kept men alive.
It did not make them free.

This distinction matters.

Because when Black men fail to achieve stability through hustle alone, the failure is framed as personal inadequacy instead of structural design.

The Hustle-Syndrome was never meant to be permanent.
It was meant to manage containment.

And once it served that function, it would be used as evidence—proof that Black men were unstable, reckless, or incapable of discipline.

A system that creates desperation, then condemns the behavior desperation produces, is not neutral.

It is strategic.

The Hustle-Syndrome was not a cultural flaw.

It was a survival language learned in an environment that refused to speak opportunity fluently.

CHAPTER 15

Drugs, Alcohol, and the Flooding of the Community

Drugs did not arrive in Black communities by accident.
Alcohol did not become normalized by coincidence.
And addiction did not explode because of moral collapse.

What happened was not random exposure.
It was managed saturation.

By the time drugs became visible, the groundwork had already been laid.
Black men had been locked out of stable employment.
Fathers had been pushed out of homes.
Political power had been stripped.
Economic mobility had been obstructed.

Survival had already been criminalized.

Drugs entered environments where stability had been intentionally weakened.
They did not create chaos.
They fed on chaos that already existed.

Alcohol had long been the first tool.
It dulled pain.
It softened anger.
It blurred memory.
It kept men functional enough to work, but numb enough not to organize.

This pattern was not new.
Alcohol had been used during slavery, during Reconstruction, and through Jim Crow as a socially acceptable sedative.

It was legal.
It was accessible.
And it carried no political cost.

But alcohol alone was not enough.

As economic pressure increased and informal survival economies grew, something else was introduced—something far more profitable, far more criminalizing, and far more useful for control.

Drugs.

Not as a medical crisis.
Not as a public health failure.
But as a jurisdictional weapon.

By the late 20th century, the state reframed addiction as criminality and positioned Black men at the center of the narrative.
This framing did not emerge organically.
It was chosen.

In 1971, President Richard Nixon officially declared drug abuse "public enemy number one."
The public explanation was protection.
The private strategy was disruption.

Years later, John Ehrlichman—one of Nixon's top advisors—admitted what had been understood internally at the time: the administration associated heroin with Black communities and marijuana with anti-war activists, then built policy around those associations.
The goal was never health.

The goal was control.

This matters because it establishes intent.

Once drugs were framed as a moral crisis instead of a structural one, enforcement could replace investment.
Punishment could replace treatment.
Surveillance could replace opportunity.

And Black men became the default targets.

The legal architecture shifted rapidly.

During the 1970s and accelerating through the 1980s under President Ronald Reagan, Congress passed a series of laws that transformed drug enforcement into a pipeline to prison.
Mandatory minimum sentencing laws stripped judges of discretion.
Context disappeared.
Rehabilitation was removed from the conversation.

A judge could no longer say, *"This man deserves help."*
The law said, *"Send him away."*

These laws were not applied evenly.

Crack cocaine—more prevalent in poor, urban communities—was punished at dramatically harsher rates than powder cocaine, which was more common in wealthier, white communities.

For years, possession of crack carried penalties 100 times more severe than powder cocaine.

This was not chemistry.
This was not pharmacology.
This was policy.

A Black man caught with a small amount of crack could receive the same sentence as a white man caught with one hundred times more powder cocaine.

That disparity was not accidental.
It was legislated.

At the same time, law enforcement funding models changed. Departments began receiving federal money based on arrest numbers, drug seizures, and asset forfeiture.
Volume became success.
Fairness became irrelevant.

Black neighborhoods were flooded with police.

Not counselors.
Not social workers.
Not job programs.
Police.

Entire communities of Black men were placed under constant surveillance as a normal condition of life.

If you are watched more, you are stopped more.
If you are stopped more, you are searched more.
If you are searched more, you are arrested more.
If you are arrested more, you are recorded more.

And those records then justified even more surveillance.

This created a closed loop.

Black men became statistical products of their own over-policing.

But the damage went deeper than incarceration.

Mass incarceration did not simply remove men from the street. It removed them from their timelines.

A man in prison does not build wealth.
He does not parent daily.
He does not form career networks.
He does not stabilize his household.

Years of a man's most productive life were placed behind concrete and steel.

And when he returned, he returned marked.

That record followed him everywhere.

Jobs denied.
Housing denied.
Licenses denied.
Voting rights stripped in many states.
Dignity questioned permanently.

Punishment did not end at release.
It multiplied.

This produced a new identity in American life: the permanently suspicious Black man.

Even men who never touched drugs were affected—by geography, by association, by proximity.
Children grew up watching patrol cars instead of fathers.
Women carried households alone.
Communities normalized absence.

And still, the national story insisted this was a crime problem.

Not a design problem.
Not a policy problem.
Not a targeting problem.

Psychologically, the War on Drugs reshaped Black masculinity under conditions of fear and constant watch.

You cannot be soft.
You cannot be visible.
You cannot trust institutions.
You cannot call policc.
You cannot admit vulnerability.

Because you are always being watched.

Hypervigilance became intelligence.
Guardedness became dignity.
Silence became survival.

These were not peace traits.
They were survival traits.

The prison system itself became a continuation of the same conditioning.

Violence hierarchies.
Silence codes.
Emotional suppression.
Constant threat assessment.

Men came home trained to survive danger, not to build peace.

And then society demanded they reenter as calm, trusting citizens without addressing what had been done to them.

That demand was dishonest.

The War on Drugs did not fail.

It worked exactly as designed.

It removed men.
It fractured families.
It expanded prisons.
It justified policing budgets.
It normalized surveillance.
It criminalized survival.

And the most painful truth is this:

The government knew these policies disproportionately affected Black men.

Reports showed it.
Statistics proved it.
Commissions acknowledged it.

But the machine kept running.

Because once a system becomes profitable—politically, economically, and socially—it does not dismantle itself willingly.

This was never a war on substances.

It was a war on autonomy.

And Black men were positioned directly in its path.

What followed next was predictable.

Once drugs provided justification, the state moved to neutralize anything that looked like resistance or self-defense.

Which is why the next chapter is not about crime.

It is about retaliation.

And why gun laws, prison expansion, and permanent exclusion followed immediately after.

The flood was never accidental.

It was managed.

And the consequences were calculated.

CHAPTER 16

The Black Panthers and Gun Law Retaliation

When Black men organized discipline, the rules changed.

The Black Panther Party did not terrify America because it was chaotic. It terrified America because it was structured. Its members were not roaming gangs. They were trained, educated, uniformed, and politically conscious. They studied law. They studied history. They understood their rights—and they exercised them deliberately.

This was unacceptable.

At a time when Black communities were being flooded with drugs and destabilized from within, the Panthers represented the opposite of what the system wanted Black masculinity to look like. They were sober. They were organized. They were armed legally. They fed children. They provided medical care. They taught political literacy.

They demonstrated what happened when Black men reclaimed authority with discipline.

And that example could not be allowed to spread.

One of the most revealing moments in American history occurred in 1967, when members of the Black Panther Party marched into the California State Capitol in Sacramento. They were armed, but they were not violent. They were exercising their Second Amendment rights under existing law, openly carrying firearms to protest proposed legislation that would restrict those very rights.

Their presence exposed a contradiction the country was not prepared to confront.

The Second Amendment was not written with disciplined Black men in mind.

Until that moment, open carry had been largely tolerated. But once Black men demonstrated that they understood the law, could organize collectively, and were willing to defend themselves and their communities within legal bounds, the tolerance evaporated.

The response was immediate.

California passed the Mulford Act, banning the open carry of loaded firearms. The law was supported by both Democrats and Republicans and signed by then-Governor Ronald Reagan. The message was clear: gun rights were acceptable only when they did not empower Black men.

This pattern would repeat itself.

Whenever Black men organized with discipline and legality, laws shifted to restrict them. When chaos appeared in Black communities, it was punished. When order appeared, it was feared.

Either way, control was the objective.

The Panthers understood that policing had never been neutral in Black neighborhoods. They monitored police behavior not to provoke violence, but to assert accountability. They carried law books alongside weapons. They knew exactly what was permitted.

That knowledge itself was a threat.

America was not afraid of guns.
It was afraid of Black men who understood the law and refused to be passive.

This chapter exposes a truth often obscured in public discourse: gun control in America has frequently been reactive, not preventive. It has expanded not in response to abstract violence, but in response to specific populations asserting power.

The Panthers' example revealed that Black men were not inherently disorganized or incapable of discipline. When given purpose, instruction, and structure, they built systems that protected their communities more effectively than external forces ever had.

That reality challenged every narrative used to justify exclusion.

So, the system responded the only way it knew how—by changing the rules.

After the Panthers were neutralized through infiltration, arrests, assassinations, and legal restrictions, the vacuum returned. Drugs and guns remained. Leadership was gone. Trust was fractured.

And when violence rose in the absence of structure, the blame landed squarely on Black men.

The irony is brutal.

When Black men organized lawfully, they were shut down. When Black men were left in chaos, they were criminalized.

There was no acceptable version of Black masculinity that involved autonomy.

This chapter is not about glorifying the Panthers. It is about recognizing what they represented: a glimpse of what disciplined, politically aware Black manhood could look like when it refused to submit to erasure.

That glimpse had to be extinguished.

Because a man who knows his rights, organizes his community, and protects his people disrupts every system built on fear, dependency, and fragmentation.

And once again, the lesson was reinforced:

Order will not be tolerated if it comes from you.

CHAPTER 17

Mass Incarceration

Mass incarceration did not emerge because crime suddenly increased.
It expanded because removal became policy.

By the time mass incarceration accelerated in the late 20th century, the groundwork had already been laid. Economic access had been restricted. Political power had been neutralized. Leadership had been dismantled. Informal survival economies had been criminalized.

Prison became the solution to a problem the system itself had created.

This shift was sold as public safety.
In practice, it was population control.

Legislation hardened penalties across the board. Mandatory minimums stripped judges of discretion. Truth-in-sentencing laws extended time served. Parole opportunities narrowed or vanished entirely.

Time stopped being proportional.
Punishment stopped being corrective.

A single conviction could now remove a man from society for decades—or for life—regardless of context, intent, or harm caused.

Nonviolent offenses carried violent consequences.

Possession became trafficking.
Association became conspiracy.
Prior records became multipliers.

The system did not evaluate men individually.
It processed them categorically.

Once incarcerated, Black men entered institutions that were
never designed for rehabilitation. Education programs were
underfunded or eliminated. Job training was inconsistent. Mental
health care was minimal.

Prisons managed bodies, not futures.

Release did not restore freedom.

A man exiting prison carried a permanent mark. Employment
applications demanded disclosure. Housing authorities enforced
exclusion. Professional licenses were denied. Student aid was
restricted. Voting rights were stripped in many states.

Freedom became conditional.

Mass incarceration functioned as a revolving door. Without
access to legal income, housing, or stability, recidivism became
predictable—not because men wanted to return, but because
survival pathways had been sealed.

The system then cited recidivism as proof of criminal nature.

Cause disappeared.
Effect was criminalized.

Families absorbed the impact.

Fathers vanished for years at a time. Children grew up without daily male presence. Relationships fractured under distance, stigma, and financial strain.

Incarceration did not just remove men from communities. It destabilized entire family structures.

Women carried households alone. Children learned absence as normal. Emotional connection was replaced with monitored visits and collect calls.

Love became institutionalized.

The psychological effects extended beyond prison walls. Communities under constant surveillance internalized threat. Police presence became synonymous with danger rather than protection.

A generation of Black boys grew up learning that visibility invited punishment.

Masculinity adapted.

Strength became guarded.
Emotion became liability.
Trust became risk.

And again, adaptation was misread as defect.

Mass incarceration also created economic incentives to maintain itself. Prisons generated revenue. Rural economies became dependent on prison jobs. Budgets expanded with inmate counts.

Human confinement became an industry.

Once profit entered the equation, reform slowed.

This is why mass incarceration persisted even as crime rates declined. The system no longer responded to conditions. It responded to infrastructure.

Empty cells were losses.
Full cells were success.

The narrative followed.

Black men were framed as inherently criminal. Incarceration rates were presented without context. Structural causes were omitted. Policy decisions were erased.

Statistics replaced stories.

What was never acknowledged is that no group in American history has been imprisoned at this scale without deliberate design.

Mass incarceration did not happen to Black men.
It was done to Black men.

It succeeded where earlier systems could not.

It removed men quietly.
Legally.
Permanently.

And when entire communities felt the absence, the system blamed culture instead of policy.

This chapter matters because mass incarceration is not the end of the story.

It is the mechanism that made everything that followed possible.

Once men were removed at scale,
once families were destabilized,
once survival was criminalized—

the next phase could move freely.

And it did.

CHAPTER 18

Psychological Inheritance (The Mirror Effect)

Trauma does not end when conditions change.
It adapts.

When systems persist long enough, they do not just shape behavior in one generation. They imprint patterns that are passed down—often without explanation, without language, and without awareness.

This is psychological inheritance.

The Mirror Effect is the process by which behaviors formed under pressure are reflected forward as norms, even after the original pressure has shifted form.

Black men did not simply respond to slavery, Jim Crow, economic exclusion, or mass incarceration in isolation. They adapted repeatedly—generation after generation—to survive environments that punished visibility, leadership, and stability.

Those adaptations did not disappear.
They were inherited.

A father who learned silence as protection models silence to his son.
A man who learned distance as safety teaches emotional restraint without naming it.
A boy raised without explanation mirrors behavior without context.

This is not failure.
It is transmission.

The Mirror Effect explains why patterns persist even when the original conditions are no longer visible. It explains why behaviors outlive the environments that produced them.

Survival strategies become identity.

Hypervigilance becomes "attitude."
Emotional withdrawal becomes "coldness."
Aggression becomes "defiance."
Silence becomes "absence."

These traits are often judged without understanding their origin.

A man who grew up watching authority punish honesty learns discretion.
A man who watched his father removed learns impermanence.
A man raised in instability learns control—or chaos—as regulation.

The nervous system adapts first.
Language comes later—if at all.

This is why instruction gaps matter.

When men are not taught *why* they behave the way they do, behavior becomes instinct rather than choice. Reflex replaces reflection.

The Mirror Effect does not require conscious intent.
It operates through proximity.

Children study tone before words.
They learn safety by observation.
They absorb regulation patterns long before they understand explanation.

A boy learns how to be a man by watching how men respond under pressure.

If pressure is constant, regulation becomes rigid.

This is how generational cycles form without deliberate teaching.

A man who learned to suppress emotion may genuinely love his children, yet struggle to express warmth consistently. His children may interpret that restraint as distance—even though it was never intended as absence.

The mirror reflects behavior, not motivation.

This effect is compounded by absence.

When fathers are removed physically or psychologically, sons inherit fragments instead of frameworks. Masculinity becomes assembled from partial images—media, peers, enforcement, threat.

Manhood becomes reactive instead of instructed.

This is where misinterpretation begins.

Black men are often judged as emotionally unavailable without acknowledging that emotional visibility has historically been punished. They are criticized for guardedness without recognizing that openness once invited danger.

Adaptation is mistaken for pathology.

The Mirror Effect also explains gender tension.

Women raised amid instability often learn hyper-independence as safety. Men raised amid removal often learn withdrawal as protection. When these patterns meet in relationships, conflict emerges—not from lack of care, but from mismatched survival languages.

One seeks reassurance.
The other seeks containment.

Neither recognizes the pattern as inherited.

This is not individual dysfunction.
It is historical residue.

The Mirror Effect does not absolve responsibility.

It explains context.

Understanding inheritance creates choice.
Unexamined inheritance becomes destiny.

This chapter matters because healing cannot occur without recognition.

You cannot break a cycle you believe is personality.
You cannot correct behavior you do not understand.
You cannot change patterns you have never named.

Black men have been carrying psychological adaptations mistaken for identity.

Once those adaptations are seen clearly—not judged, not romanticized, not excused—they can be interrupted.

The Mirror Effect is not permanent.

Inheritance can be examined.
Patterns can be edited.
Transmission can be redirected.

But only if the mirror is acknowledged.

Otherwise, history continues to speak through behavior—long after its original voice has gone silent.

CHAPTER 19

The Long Silence

Silence did not begin as apathy.
It began as protection.

After generations of punishment for speaking, organizing,
resisting, or standing visibly, silence became strategy. Not
because Black men had nothing to say—but because saying it
often carried consequences.

Silence was learned.

A man who watched leaders killed learned discretion.
A man who watched fathers removed learned restraint.
A man who watched success punished learned invisibility.

Over time, silence stopped being situational.
It became cultural.

This was not the absence of thought.
It was the management of risk.

Speaking too loudly could cost a job.
Speaking too clearly could invite surveillance.
Speaking too often could mark a man as "trouble."

So Black men learned when to speak—and more importantly,
when not to.

The Long Silence is what happens when survival requires constant self-censorship.

It shaped how Black men moved in workplaces, schools, courts, and public spaces. It taught men to choose their words carefully, to avoid confrontation even when wronged, to swallow frustration rather than escalate.

This silence was later misinterpreted.

Quiet became disengagement.
Caution became indifference.
Restraint became absence.

But silence does not mean emptiness.
It means calculation.

The Long Silence also affected political participation.

After decades of terror around voting, organizing, and leadership, many Black men learned that visibility invited retaliation. Participation felt dangerous. Silence felt safer.

This is how disengagement is manufactured.

You do not have to outlaw speech if you punish it consistently enough.

The Long Silence also shaped emotional expression.

When Black men learned early that vulnerability could be exploited, emotion was managed privately or not at all. Pain was internalized. Fear was disguised. Grief was postponed.

This did not eliminate emotion.
It redirected it.

Unspoken pain does not disappear.
It accumulates.

The Long Silence is why anger sometimes appears without
warning. It is why emotional expression can feel delayed,
compressed, or explosive. It is why some men struggle to
articulate feelings they have been trained to suppress.

Silence becomes storage.

And storage has limits.

This silence was reinforced institutionally.

In schools, Black boys learned that speaking up invited
discipline.
In courts, Black men learned that explaining themselves rarely
changed outcomes.
In workplaces, Black men learned that voicing concern could
stall advancement.

So, silence became professionalism.
Silence became maturity.
Silence became "knowing how the world works."

And then the narrative flipped.

The same system that punished speech later criticized silence.
Black men were labeled emotionally unavailable, politically
disengaged, and socially distant—without acknowledging the
history that trained those behaviors.

The Long Silence was not chosen freely.
It was conditioned.

It also fractured community transmission.

When men stop speaking openly, wisdom is not passed down clearly. Lessons become implicit. Warnings become vague. Guidance becomes fragmented.

Sons inherit behavior without explanation.

This is how confusion deepens.

A boy watches silence without understanding its origin. He may replicate it without knowing what it protects him from—or what it costs him.

The Long Silence also created internal isolation.

When men do not speak openly to one another, trust weakens. Brotherhood becomes symbolic instead of functional. Men carry burdens privately instead of sharing load collectively.

This isolation is not preference.
It is inheritance.

The system benefits from this silence.

Silence prevents coordination.
Silence limits resistance.
Silence keeps pain individualized instead of systemic.

A man who believes his struggle is personal will not challenge structural causes.

This is why silence persisted even as conditions shifted.

But silence is not neutral.

What is not named cannot be healed.
What is not spoken cannot be examined.
What remains silent continues to operate unchecked.

The Long Silence protected Black men for a time.

But protection has a cost.

It delayed healing.
It fragmented communication.
It obscured truth.

This chapter matters because breaking silence is not rebellion—it is repair.

Speech is not weakness.
Naming is not danger.
Clarity is not threat.

Silence served its purpose.
But its season has passed.

If the next generations are to inherit something different, the silence must be understood—not condemned, not romanticized, not ignored.

Only then can it be released.

Only then can voice replace vigilance.

Only then can truth move freely—without fear.

A Letter to America

Dear America,

This is not a scream.

This is not a threat.

This is not a demand.

This is a mirror.

You have spent centuries asking Black men to explain themselves without ever explaining yourself. You have asked us to justify our pain while pretending your systems were neutral. You have asked us to perform calm while you performed erasure.

This chapter exists because denial has had too much comfort.

You like to say that what happened is over.
That it's history.
That it isn't "like that anymore."

But systems don't disappear because language changes. They disappear when architecture changes. And very little of your architecture has been rebuilt.

You did not simply "have" slavery.
You financed it.
You insured it.
You governed it.
You taxed it.

You did not simply "experience" segregation.
You legalized it.
You defended it.
You enforced it.
You normalized it.

You did not simply "deal with" Black communities.
You mapped them.
You starved them.
You flooded them with police.
You criminalized them.
You surveilled them.

This is not accusation.

This is historical accounting.

You cannot ask a people to move forward while pretending you never pushed them backward.

You have taught generations of Black men that their anger is dangerous but have never acknowledged the violence that produced it.

You have demanded we respect laws that were written to contain us.

You have expected loyalty from men your system never made safe.

You point to "progress" without addressing foundation.

You celebrate individual Black success stories while ignoring the systems designed to prevent them from existing.

You use the word "opportunity" while ignoring infrastructure.

You have mastered the language of innocence.

But innocence is not declared.

It is demonstrated.

This chapter is not written to shame you.

It is written to expose you to yourself.

Because denial is not neutral.

Denial is active.

Denial protects architecture.

Denial maintains imbalance.

Denial keeps the comfort of those who benefit from silence.

Here is the truth you avoid:

Black men did not break America.

Black men were broken by America.

Not because you hated us.

But because you did not need to love us to use us.

You needed us strong enough to build your economy
but not strong enough to challenge your structure.

That is not emotional.

That is mechanical.

You say, "Why can't you just get over it?"

Because wounds that were never acknowledged were never
closed.

You say, "That was generations ago."

But the systems those generations built are still standing.

Banks still reflect redlining damage.
Schools still reflect segregated funding.
Neighborhoods still reflect mapped poverty.
Prisons still reflect targeted policy.
Police still reflect occupation psychology.

This is not decoration.

This is foundation.

You cannot decorate a house with cracked walls and call it
repair.

You must rebuild.

Not with apologies.

With intention.

With policy.

With acknowledgment.

With truth.

This is not about revenge.

This is about integrity.

A country that cannot be honest about its construction cannot be honest about its future.

If you want Black men to trust, you must become trustworthy.

If you want dignity, you must practice it.

If you want peace, you must build it.

We have carried your silence quietly for generations.

We are no longer required to.

And we are no longer asking permission to name what is real.

This is not radical.

This is accurate.

And accuracy is what justice begins with.

SECTION II — THE PERSONAL
Forgiveness — From My Perspective

CHAPTER 20

The Man I Became Without Knowing Why

I did not wake up one day and decide who I would be.

I became him quietly.
Through repetition.
Through pressure.
Through what worked.

I learned early how to read rooms.
How to feel tension before it spoke.
How to stay alert without looking afraid.
How to move without drawing attention.

No one called it training.
But that's what it was.

I was not taught manhood.
I was taught endurance.

I was not shown how to lead.
I was shown how to survive systems that did not explain
themselves.

I learned what *not* to do long before I learned what to build.
I learned what attracted punishment.
What invited scrutiny.
What made life harder than it already was.

So, I adjusted.

I became efficient.
I became guarded.
I became self-reliant in ways that looked like strength and felt
like isolation.

And for a long time, I thought this was identity.

I thought this was just who I was.

It never occurred to me that I had become a man in response to something, not in alignment with myself.

The Shift

There comes a moment—quiet, unannounced—when survival stops feeling like success.

Nothing is falling apart on the outside.
But nothing feels grounded on the inside.

You are functioning.
You are producing.
You are holding things together.

And yet, something is missing.

Not motivation.
Not discipline.

Orientation.

You realize you have learned how to move, but not how to rest.
How to react, but not how to choose.
How to endure pressure, but not how to define peace.

That was the moment I began to ask a dangerous question:

Why am I like this?

Not *what happened to me.*
Not *who failed me.*

But *what shaped me when I wasn't looking.*

That question opens a door most men were never given permission to walk through.

The Man Inside the System

The most dangerous prison in America is not made of steel.

It is made of expectations.

By the time a Black man reaches adulthood, he has absorbed an unspoken curriculum.
No syllabus.
No warning.

Only consequence.

He learns how he is seen before he learns who he is.
He learns the weight of his skin before the depth of his mind.
He learns when to soften and when to harden—not by choice, but by survival.

This chapter is not about policy.

It is about interior architecture.

What happens inside a man raised in systems that never allowed him to rest?

Most Black men do not wake up thinking, *I will be angry today.*

They wake up scanning.

They read rooms.
Clock exits.
Watch faces.
Measure tone.

This is not paranoia.

It is training without consent.

When vigilance becomes routine, identity becomes reactive.

A man stops asking, *who am I?*
He starts asking, *how do I avoid harm?*
How do I stay unnoticed?
How do I move without becoming a target?

That constant calculation becomes muscle memory.

Muscle memory becomes posture.
Posture becomes personality.

And the world mistakes survival for character.

Black men are labeled distant, cold, intimidating,
unapproachable—without ever asking the honest question:

What kind of environment produces this stance?

You cannot grow openness in a battlefield.
You cannot grow vulnerability in a cage.
You cannot grow softness in a system that weaponizes it.

Inside many Black men, there is a war that never announces
itself.

One side wants peace.
The other is addicted to armor.

One side wants connection.
The other does not trust safety.

One side wants to build.
The other is exhausted.

And exhaustion hardens people.

Fragmentation

There is also the cost of split identity.

In white spaces, the Black man is told to be calm, agreeable,
non-threatening,

In Black spaces, he is told to be dominant, respected, unbreakable.

This is not adaptability.

It is fragmentation.

When a man learns to divide himself to survive, he loses a unified sense of self.
He becomes what the situation demands.

Over time, that creates numbness.

A man who never gets to be fully himself begins to doubt that a "self" exists at all.

He performs competence.
He performs strength.
He performs control.

But he does not feel at home inside himself.

Silent Grief

There is grief here that rarely gets named.

Grief for fathers lost to absence.
Grief for brothers lost to cages.
Grief for sons walking into the same maze.
Grief for futures that were never permitted to exist.

But grief has never been treated as sacred in Black men.

It has been mocked.
Dismissed.
Weaponized.

So, grief becomes stillness.

Stillness becomes distance.

Distance gets mislabeled as emotional deficiency.

Romantic relationships fracture here.

Not because Black men do not love deeply—but because attachment has often felt unsafe.

So, love is expressed through control.
Stability through distance.
Protection through detachment.

Not because emotion is absent.

But because it is too present for a world that punishes it.

Reintroduction

This chapter matters because it reveals something often ignored:

The Black man is not empty.

He is full.

Full of memory.
Full of pressure.
Full of restraint.

The system did not make him heartless.

It made him cautious.
Strategic.
Defensive.

Those are not moral failures.

They are survival blueprints.

And survival blueprints are difficult to outgrow when danger never fully leaves.

But here is the truth that changes everything:

Inside many Black men, there is still a memory older than fear.

A memory of structure.
A memory of grounded masculinity.
A memory of dignity that does not require hardness.

That memory never disappeared.

It went quiet.

This book is not about blaming the system.

It is about guiding that memory back into awareness.

Because the man inside the system does not need to be saved.

He needs to be reintroduced to himself.

CHAPTER 21

Growing Up Without a Map

I did not grow up without direction.
I grew up without translation.

The rules were everywhere, but none of them were explained.
What to avoid was clear.
What to build was not.

I learned early how to read danger.
How to scan a room.
How to lower my voice.
How to stand without drawing attention.
How to harden when softness felt risky.

No one ever sat me down and said, *this is manhood.*
They showed me survival instead.

And survival, when repeated long enough, starts to feel like identity.

I did not know that what I was learning was adaptive.
I thought it was natural.
I thought this was just how men like me were.

That is how most boys grow up when guidance has been replaced with pressure.

When fathers are absent—not by choice, but by removal—boys do not become blank.
They become observant.
They study consequences instead of instruction.
They learn by watching what gets punished and what gets tolerated.

This creates a map made of warnings instead of pathways.

Don't trust too quickly.
Don't show weakness.
Don't stand out too much.
Don't feel too deeply.
Don't need too much.

Those rules are not spoken aloud.
They are absorbed.

And over time, they begin to look like personality.

Trauma Disguised as Culture

One of the greatest tricks ever pulled on Black men in America was the lie that our pain was our personality.

Over time, behaviors created by oppression were relabeled as identity.
Survival became style.
Armor became fashion.
Trauma became "culture."

Once that happened, the systems that caused the harm could quietly exit the conversation—while the men living with the consequences became the blame.

This is not an emotional argument.
It is a psychological one.

When trauma is repeated long enough, it stops looking like crisis and starts looking like normal.

Psychology calls this normalization of dysfunction. It happens in any population exposed to sustained threat. What makes the Black male experience distinct is not the presence of trauma—but its consistency across generations.

From slavery to Jim Crow.
From redlining to mass incarceration.
From COINTELPRO to aggressive policing.

Across centuries, the lesson remained the same:

Safety is not guaranteed.
Trust is dangerous.
Vulnerability is risky.
Visibility can cost you your life.

These are not character flaws.
They are survival laws.

But when a generation grows up knowing only survival, it begins to treat survival responses as identity traits.

Anger becomes "personality."
Emotional shutdown becomes "strength."
Detachment becomes "cool."
Hyper-independence becomes "manhood."

And the world applauds it.

Music sells it.
Movies celebrate it.
Industries monetize it.

But none of it is natural.

This is what trauma looks like when it is unnamed.

A boy whose father was removed –by prisons, policies, or death—does not grow up weak. He grows up adaptive. He learns patterns quickly. He learns how to minimize need. He learns how to detach before attachment can become pain.

This kind of emotional armor makes sense.

But it has consequences.

A man who never learned safety does not know how to relax.
A man who never learned stable love does not know how to trust intimacy.
A man who never learned protection does not know how to give it without control.

The world began calling these outcomes "toxic masculinity" without context. But without context, the label becomes another form of erasure.

You cannot criticize the weapon without naming the war.

This is not about excusing behavior.
Accountability still matters.

But accountability without context is just punishment with better language.

People observe outcomes without tracing origin.

They see emotionally distant fathers.
Aggressive young men.
Guarded husbands.
Conflicted relationships.

And they call it culture.

But culture is created.

And this version of culture was forged inside a laboratory of pressure.

Black men were never taught how to be soft safely—because softness was punished.
Never taught how to express emotion—because expression was dangerous.
Never taught how to be vulnerable—because vulnerability made us targets.

Those lessons do not vanish when laws change.

They live in posture.
In tone.
In reflex.

This is trauma having children.

When stable male presence is removed from homes, emotional labor shifts. Women are forced to carry what was never meant to be carried alone. Boys grow up learning masculinity from peers instead of elders, from survival instead of structure.

That does not make them deficient.

It makes their masculinity reactionary rather than rooted.

It shows up as performative toughness.
Emotional withdrawal.
Status-driven respect.
Fear of vulnerability.

Again—not culture.

Conditioning.

The most dangerous effect of disguising trauma as culture is that it allows the system to step back.

If this is "just how they are," then no repair is required.
No policy change.
No accountability.
No restitution.

Just judgment.

Black men were shaped by crisis—not deficiency.

And crisis, when unhealed, becomes identity.

Many Black men do not even realize they are hurting—not because they are ignorant, but because pain feels familiar. Pain becomes baseline.

When baseline is pain, peace feels suspicious.
When baseline is chaos, stability feels boring.
When baseline is betrayal, love feels unsafe.

That is not flaw.

That is conditioning.

And once trauma is named, it can be healed.

But as long as it is mislabeled, it will be punished.

Growing up without a map does not mean growing up without intelligence.

It means growing up translating danger instead of direction.

I did not lack capacity.
I lacked clarity.

I was taught what to avoid long before I was taught what to build.
I was trained to endure before I was invited to feel.
I learned how to survive systems before I learned how to live inside myself.

And like many Black men, I learned that silence was safer than explanation.

Which is why silence would beco

me the next teacher.

CHAPTER 22

Silence as Survival

Silence was never the absence of voice.
It was the presence of danger.

By the time a Black man reaches adulthood in America, he has already learned an unspoken curriculum. No one hands him a textbook. No one gives him instructions. But the lessons arrive daily—through looks, consequences, warnings, losses, and close calls.

He learns how he is seen before he learns who he is.
He learns the weight of his skin before the depth of his mind.
He learns when to soften and when to harden—not based on choice, but on survival.

Silence becomes one of the earliest tools.

Not because Black men have nothing to say.
But because speaking has consequences.

For generations, Black men learned that visibility invites scrutiny, and scrutiny invites punishment. Saying the wrong thing, saying too much, or saying anything at all could cost a job, a future, or a life. Silence was not weakness. It was calculation.

This chapter is not about policy.
It is about interior architecture.

What happens inside a man who grows up in systems that were never designed to let him rest?

Most Black men do not wake up thinking, *I will be angry today.*
They wake up scanning.

They enter rooms reading air.
They move through spaces clocking exits.
They watch faces.
They feel shifts in tone.
They calculate risk where others feel neutral.

This is not paranoia.
This is training without consent.

When survival becomes routine, identity becomes reactive. A man begins to build himself around defense instead of purpose. He stops asking, *who am I?* and starts asking, *how do I avoid pain? How do I move without being exposed? How do I exist without attracting danger?*

That constant vigilance becomes muscle memory.
And muscle memory becomes personality.

This is the quiet tragedy.

The world often describes Black men as intimidating, distant, cold, or closed off—without ever asking the only honest question: *What kind of environment produces this posture?*

You cannot grow softness in a battlefield.
You cannot grow openness in a cage.
You cannot grow vulnerability in a world that weaponizes it.

Inside many Black men raised under pressure, there is a war happening that nobody sees.

One side wants peace.
The other is addicted to armor.

One side wants love.
The other does not trust safety.

One side wants to build.
The other is exhausted.

And exhaustion hardens people.

Silence, over time, stops being something a man chooses.
It becomes something he is.

Many Black men do not speak their loneliness because loneliness has never been treated as sacred in them. It has been mocked, dismissed, minimized, or used against them. So, solitude becomes survival rather than choice.

And when solitude becomes habit, connection becomes foreign.

This is not emotional deficiency.
This is emotional adaptation.

There is also the reality of fractured identity.

The Black man inside the system is constantly navigating two worlds that demand opposite things. In white spaces, he is expected to be calm, polite, measured, agreeable, non-threatening. In Black spaces, he is expected to be strong, dominant, unbreakable, respected.

This is not flexibility.
It is fragmentation.

When a man learns to split himself in order to survive, he slowly loses a unified sense of self. He becomes a performance artist of identity—adjusting tone, posture, and expression depending on who is watching.

Over time, this creates numbness.

A man who never gets to be fully himself eventually stops believing that "self" is real. He becomes what the situation requires. That costs something.

There is also silent grief.

Grief for brothers lost to cages.
Grief for fathers lost to absence.

Grief for sons growing up inside the same maze.
Grief for futures that were never allowed to exist.

But grief is dangerous in a system that never allowed Black men to be vulnerable. So, grief turns into stillness. Stillness turns into distance. Distance gets mislabeled as coldness.

Romantic relationships suffer here deeply.

A man who has grown up watching instability learns early that attachment is risky. He does not resist love because he does not feel. He resists it because it feels unsafe. He loves through control. He stabilizes through distance. He protects through detachment.

Not because he does not care.
But because he cares too deeply for a world that punishes it.

This is where silence becomes generational.

Fathers teach sons—often without words—what survival looks like. Sons learn when to speak and when not to. They learn that asking for help invites judgment. They learn that vulnerability is expensive.

Over time, silence stops looking like protection and starts looking like identity.

The system then points to that silence as evidence of defect.

But silence was learned.
It was taught.
It was reinforced.

The system did not make Black men heartless.
It made them cautious.
It made them strategic.
It made them defensive.

These are not moral failures.
They are survival blueprints.

And survival blueprints are hard to outgrow when danger has never fully gone away.

But here is the truth that matters most.

Inside many Black men, beneath the armor, beneath the silence, beneath the vigilance, there is still a memory of something older than fear.

A memory of structure.
A memory of purpose.
A memory of grounded masculinity.
A memory of dignity that does not require hardness.

That memory is faint.
But it exists.

And this book is not about blaming the system endlessly.
It is about guiding that memory back to the surface.

Because the man inside the system does not need to be saved.

He needs to be reintroduced to himself.

CHAPTER 23

My Father

My father did not teach me manhood with speeches.
He taught it with behavior.

This was not neglect.
It was inheritance.

For Black men of his generation, explanation was rarely modeled
as safety. They were raised in environments where authority was
conditional, vulnerability was punished, and questioning systems
invited consequence. Survival depended on endurance, not
articulation.

So, men showed more than they said.

My father carried responsibility without language. He worked.
He showed up physically. He absorbed pressure quietly. Love
was expressed through consistency, provision, and presence—
not through emotional narration.

That was the model available to him.

Historically, Black fathers were not encouraged to explain
themselves. They were expected to perform. Emotional
transparency carried risk—at work, in public, and often even at
home. A man who explained too much could be misunderstood.
A man who complained too much could be labeled unstable. A
man who questioned too openly could be targeted.

Silence was safer.

So, my father modeled manhood through action. Strength meant reliability. Discipline meant restraint. Care meant sacrifice. These lessons were real, valuable, and incomplete.

He was present in ways that mattered and distant in ways that were structural.

This distance was not absence.
It was armor.

Black fathers of his era learned to protect their families by limiting exposure. They believed stability came from minimizing conflict, not unpacking emotion. Their authority came from consistency, not conversation.

They were not taught how to translate internal pressure into language.

This matters because boys learn by observation. When instruction is absent, behavior becomes curriculum. I learned how to endure. I learned how to work. I learned how to stay composed under pressure.

What I did not learn—because it was not demonstrated—was how to articulate uncertainty, fear, or emotional need without feeling compromised.

That gap did not come from indifference.
It came from context.

Historically, Black fathers were denied the luxury of emotional exploration. Their primary responsibility was survival—first their own, then their families'. Reflection was secondary. Healing was postponed. Processing was optional at best.

The system did not reward introspection in Black men.
It rewarded compliance, productivity, and silence.

So, my father survived.

And in surviving, he passed down what survival required.

Over time, I began to recognize patterns. The way I withdrew
under stress. The way I defaulted to stoicism. The way I avoided
emotional exposure while still carrying deep responsibility.

That recognition was not accusation.
It was lineage.

Men can only pass down what they have processed. Anything
unresolved is transmitted as behavior rather than instruction.
This is how patterns persist without intention.

My father was not emotionally distant because he lacked care.
He was emotionally contained because that was how men stayed
intact in a world that scrutinized Black masculinity aggressively.

Understanding this reframed everything.

I stopped interpreting silence as absence.
I began to see it as adaptation.

This does not erase consequence. Emotional gaps still affect
sons. Distance still shapes relationships. But explanation changes
where responsibility begins.

My father did not fail me.
He was interrupted.

His generation was taught to endure, not examine. To provide, not process. To protect, not expose. That model worked in hostile systems—but it was never meant to be complete.

The danger comes when adaptation becomes doctrine.

Honoring Black fathers does not mean pretending their limitations did not matter. It means recognizing that those limitations were produced under pressure—not neglect.

Healing lineage is not rejection.
It is completion.

Carrying forward discipline, presence, and responsibility—while adding language, reflection, and emotional availability—is not betrayal of the past. It is correction of interruption.

That is how manhood evolves without erasing its roots.

And that evolution begins not with blame—but with understanding where silence came from, why it worked, and why it can no longer be the only option.

CHAPTER 24

Love Without Language

For many Black men, love was never taught as something you explained.
It was taught as something you did.

This was not emotional deficiency.
It was historical conditioning.

In environments shaped by surveillance, punishment, and instability, articulation carried risk. Saying too much could be misinterpreted. Explaining yourself could be used against you. Silence, restraint, and action became safer currencies than language.

So, love was demonstrated through labor.

Men worked longer hours.
They showed up consistently.
They fixed what was broken.
They absorbed pressure quietly.

Care was proven through endurance, not expression.

This pattern did not emerge randomly. It developed under conditions where Black men were denied emotional safety. Under slavery, fathers could not guarantee protection. Under Jim Crow, visible emotion invited vulnerability. Under economic containment, provision mattered more than explanation.

Over time, action replaced articulation.

Love became synonymous with responsibility.

A man believed that if he stayed, worked, and provided, his care would be understood without narration. He assumed presence spoke clearly enough.

But action without language leaves interpretation to the receiver.

And interpretation fills silence with fear.

Psychologically, human bonding requires reassurance and clarity. Attachment is reinforced not only by consistency, but by verbal confirmation—by naming intent, commitment, and emotional availability. When language is absent, the nervous system fills the gap.

Silence is rarely received as neutrality.
It is often received as distance.

This is where misalignment forms.

A man raised to show love through action may believe he is being dependable, steady, and mature. The person receiving that love may experience uncertainty, emotional isolation, or insecurity—not because effort is lacking, but because access is limited.

This is not incompatibility of care.
It is incompatibility of translation.

Historically, Black men were taught that composure was strength. Emotional exposure was framed as liability. Vulnerability was equated with loss of control. These lessons did not disappear in intimate relationships.

They followed men home.

So, when pressure increased, many men withdrew inward instead of outward. They solved problems instead of naming feelings. They defaulted to logic over emotion. They sought resolution instead of connection.

This approach works in systems.
It fails in intimacy.

Relationships do not require fixing.
They require feeling.

The absence of language does not mean the absence of love. But love without language places the burden of interpretation on the other person—often unfairly.

This dynamic has structural roots.

Black men were historically expected to perform masculinity without instruction. They were punished for missteps but rarely guided through emotional literacy. The result was competence without communication.

This gap produces predictable outcomes.

Silence becomes mistaken for indifference.
Restraint becomes mistaken for avoidance.
Self-protection becomes mistaken for lack of care.

Over time, trust erodes—not because love is missing, but because clarity is.

Learning to articulate love requires unlearning survival reflexes. It requires trusting that honesty will not be punished. That naming fear will not be used as leverage. That vulnerability will not result in loss of authority.

That trust was historically unsafe for Black men.

So many never practiced it.

This chapter is not an indictment.
It is diagnosis.

Love without language is incomplete—not because action is insufficient, but because human connection requires shared meaning. Words anchor intent. They reduce uncertainty. They create emotional safety.

When love is only shown and never named, it leaves room for doubt to grow—especially under stress.

The cost of this pattern is not abstract. It appears in relationships strained by misunderstanding, in partners who feel unseen despite effort, and in men who feel unappreciated despite sacrifice.

The solution is not abandonment of action.
It is expansion of expression.

Love must be demonstrated.
But it must also be spoken.

That capacity does not weaken manhood.
It stabilizes it.

And learning that distinction—between effort and explanation—is a necessary step in rebuilding relationships shaped by endurance rather than intimacy.

CHAPTER 25

The Woman Who Reflected My Wounds

Some relationships are not formed to last.
They are formed to reveal.

This is not romantic language.
It is psychological reality.

Human beings are drawn—often unconsciously—to familiarity.
Not health. Familiarity. What feels recognizable to the nervous
system is interpreted as safety, even when that recognition is
rooted in unresolved trauma.

For Black men shaped by absence, restraint, and survival-based
masculinity, connection often forms around shared adaptation
rather than shared healing.

That is where reflection begins.

The woman who reflects a man's wounds does not create them.
She activates what is already there. Her presence exposes
patterns that were previously manageable in isolation but become
visible in intimacy.

This dynamic is not personal failure.
It is patterned interaction.

Historically, Black men entered relationships carrying armor
rather than language. Emotional restraint, silence, and control
were not personality traits—they were survival strategies refined
under conditions where vulnerability invited harm.

At the same time, Black women entered relationships carrying hyper-responsibility. They were conditioned to anticipate absence, manage instability, and prepare for disappointment—not because they desired independence, but because necessity demanded it.

When these two adaptive systems meet, tension is inevitable.

A man withdraws to regulate pressure.
A woman leans in to regulate uncertainty.

Both responses are protective.
Both trigger the other.

The man experiences questioning as threat.
The woman experiences silence as abandonment.

Neither is wrong.
Both are responding to history.

This is how relational cycles form.

Silence escalates anxiety.
Anxiety escalates withdrawal.
Withdrawal confirms fear.
Fear intensifies pursuit.

The cycle tightens—not because of malice, but because neither party was taught how to interrupt it.

This pattern is frequently misdiagnosed as incompatibility or toxicity. In reality, it is misalignment between two survival strategies operating without shared language.

This chapter requires precision.

This is not a critique of Black women.

Black women have historically absorbed extraordinary responsibility—often serving simultaneously as nurturers, disciplinarians, providers, and protectors. They adapted under conditions where male presence was destabilized by policy, violence, incarceration, and economic exclusion.

They taught values.
They taught discipline.
They taught resilience.

What they could not teach—because no woman can—was male identity.

This is not indictment.
It is biological and social reality.

Across cultures and species, male development requires male modeling. Masculine regulation—how to channel strength, navigate authority, integrate vulnerability, and lead without domination—is learned through observation and correction by other men.

The absence of that modeling was not maternal failure.
It was engineered removal.

When men and women meet carrying the consequences of that removal, relationships become sites of projection rather than connection.

A man expects silence to be understood as care.
A woman expects vulnerability to signal commitment.

Neither expectation is unreasonable.
Both are historically conditioned.

Without awareness, the relationship becomes defensive.

Love turns into negotiation.
Affection turns into reassurance-seeking.
Presence turns into monitoring.

Each partner responds to symptoms rather than origins.

This is how wounds speak to wounds.

The woman who reflects a man's wounds is not his enemy. She is a mirror. She reveals where survival strategies are colliding with intimacy requirements.

The pain that emerges is not proof of failure.
It is information.

But information without interpretation leads to repetition.

Historically, Black men were punished for introspection. Reflection was framed as weakness. Emotional examination was treated as indulgence rather than necessity. As a result, many men entered relationships without the tools required to translate internal experience into shared understanding.

So, effort increased while clarity remained absent.

This imbalance creates resentment on both sides.

The man feels unrecognized for what he carries.
The woman feels unseen for what she endures.

Neither feels safe enough to slow the cycle.

Breaking this pattern requires historical literacy—not blame.

It requires understanding that relational conflict is often inherited, not invented. That attraction can form around shared injury rather than shared readiness. That chemistry is not evidence of compatibility.

This chapter is not about assigning fault.
It is about naming dynamics.

Until Black men understand how history shaped their emotional reflexes, they will continue to misinterpret relational friction as personal inadequacy or external betrayal.

And until those reflexes are interrupted consciously, the same mirrors will keep appearing—different faces, same patterns.

Healing begins when a man stops asking why a woman doesn't understand him and starts asking what he was never taught to explain.

That shift does not guarantee reconciliation.

But it does guarantee clarity.

And clarity is the prerequisite for change.

CHAPTER 26

Accountability

Accountability is often misunderstood as blame.
Historically, it has been weaponized that way.

For Black men, accountability has rarely been paired with
authority, access, or protection. It has been demanded without
power and enforced without fairness. This distortion matters—
because responsibility without agency is not accountability. It is
control.

True accountability requires three elements:
Authority.
Access.
Consequence.

When any one of these is removed, accountability collapses into
punishment.

From slavery forward, Black men were held responsible for
outcomes they did not control. Expected to labor without
ownership. To provide without access. To lead without authority.
When outcomes failed—as they were engineered to fail—the
failure was personalized.

This conditioning reshaped how accountability was internalized.

For many Black men, accountability became associated with
danger. Admitting fault invited punishment, not correction.
Vulnerability exposed weakness, not growth. Silence became
safer than honesty.

This is not character failure.
It is learned behavior.

In environments where mistakes carry irreversible consequences, survival requires minimizing exposure. Accountability becomes selective. Admissions are measured. Transparency is rationed.

Over time, this produces a fractured relationship with responsibility.

A man may carry deep internal accountability—self-critique, guilt, self-surveillance—while outwardly resisting correction. To observers, this looks like deflection or avoidance. Internally, it is self-protection.

This distinction is critical.

Many Black men do not lack accountability.
They lack safe environments in which to practice it.

Historically, accountability was enforced externally—through violence, incarceration, and humiliation—rather than cultivated internally through mentorship, correction, and restoration.

Correction without restoration teaches nothing.

This pattern followed Black men into modern institutions.

In schools, Black boys are disciplined more harshly for the same behaviors as their peers. In workplaces, mistakes are remembered longer and forgiven less readily. In the legal system, accountability becomes permanent branding.

A single error can erase a lifetime of effort.

This reality alters behavior.

Risk-taking decreases.
Transparency decreases.
Trust decreases.

A man who believes accountability equals erasure will prioritize self-preservation over self-examination.

This carries into relationships.

Partners may demand accountability without recognizing the historical weight attached to that demand. What sounds like a request for honesty can register as threat. What feels like an opportunity for growth can feel like exposure.

The result is resistance—not because accountability is rejected, but because punishment is anticipated.

This is where the conversation must mature.

Accountability does not mean absorbing blame for structural harm.
It does not mean accepting narratives that ignore context.
And it does not mean self-erasure.

True accountability is alignment between behavior, intention, and consequence—within a system that allows repair.

For Black men, reclaiming accountability requires redefining it.

It begins internally.

A man must separate responsibility from shame.
Error from identity.
Correction from annihilation.

This is difficult work—because shame was historically imposed, not chosen.

Externally, accountability requires boundaries.

A man cannot be accountable to systems that deny him fairness. He cannot be responsible for outcomes he is legally barred from influencing. Responsibility without reciprocity is exploitation.

This is not excuse-making.
It is structural realism.

Accountability also requires male spaces.

Historically, accountability among men was communal and corrective. Elders intervened early. Peers enforced standards. Consequences were proportional and restorative.

The removal of these spaces left accountability to institutions ill-equipped to teach it.

When accountability is outsourced to punishment systems, growth stops.

This chapter is not a defense against responsibility.
It is a reclamation of it.

Black men must hold themselves accountable—to their words, actions, and impact. But that accountability must be grounded in truth, not inherited shame.

A man cannot heal what he refuses to examine.
But he also cannot examine what threatens his survival.

Restoring accountability means rebuilding environments where honesty is met with correction, not destruction. Where failure invites guidance, not exile. Where responsibility leads to growth, not erasure.

Until then, accountability will continue to be demanded loudly—and practiced quietly, if at all.

And silence will continue to be mistaken for indifference.

Accountability is not about punishment.
It is about alignment.

And alignment is impossible without safety.

CHAPTER 27

I'm Not My Brother's Keeper!

That sentence didn't start with us.
It was taught to us.

Long before contracts, before agents, before record deals and endorsement checks, Black men were taught—systematically—not to trust one another. Brotherhood was framed as risk. Unity was portrayed as liability. Cooperation was treated as danger.

And it started early.

Even on the plantation, there was always one man offered a little more in exchange for betrayal. A larger portion of food. A lighter workload. Proximity to the master. Safety—temporary and conditional.

That man became the eyes and ears.

This was not accidental. It was strategy.

If you can convince one man to sell out the others, you don't need chains for everyone. You only need fear and incentive. You fracture trust at the root. You make solidarity dangerous. You teach men that survival comes from proximity to power, not loyalty to each other.

That lesson stuck.

As Black men began sneaking through cracks—after sharecropping, during the Great Migration, in northern cities, in music, in business, in athletics—the same tactic reappeared with a new suit on.

White America learned quickly: outright theft created resistance. So, theft evolved.

Patents were taken.
Music was signed away.
Land was "managed."
Ideas were "represented."
Profits were "handled."

White men no longer needed to openly steal. They learned how to finesse.

Managers arrived.
Agents arrived.
Caretakers arrived.

They spoke a language of opportunity and protection. They positioned themselves as bridges—*You need someone like me to navigate this world.* And in many cases, Black men believed them. Not because they were foolish, but because history had taught them that systems were hostile and representation felt safer than confrontation.

What wasn't explained was the cost.

Through slick contracts and legal language, Black men signed away ownership of their creations, their labor, their futures. Music catalogs. Publishing rights. Trademarks. Land deeds. Royalties.

And when Black men questioned it, they were reminded of the risk of going it alone.

You can't trust your own people.
They'll steal from you.
They're jealous.
They don't know how this world works.

That lie was reinforced deliberately.

As Black athletes rose to prominence—especially in the NBA, NFL, and MLB—the same pattern repeated. Today, over 85% of professional athletes in those leagues are Black. Yet ownership remains overwhelmingly white. Major sports brands remain almost entirely white-owned, with very few exceptions.

Black men played the game.
White men owned the infrastructure.

Agents and managers positioned themselves as saviors. They offered early money—cars, homes, small advances to families still struggling. And in exchange, they secured control over future earnings.

Not partnership.
Control.

Young men coming from poverty were taught that their pathway forward depended on these relationships. That loyalty to the agent mattered more than loyalty to community. That investing in Black businesses was risky. That surrounding themselves with other Black men invited trouble.

They were told who not to trust.

At the same time, they were encouraged to assimilate. To socialize in white spaces. To uplift white families. To invest in white businesses. To marry into whiteness. To distance themselves from the environments that produced them.

Blackness became something to escape, not reinvest in.

This was not accidental cultural drift.
It was instruction.

And when Black men did attempt to reinvest—to build for their families or communities—they were warned against it. Lawsuits appeared. Mismanagement was alleged. Scandals were publicized. Failures were amplified.

Every misstep was used as evidence.

See? We told you dealing with your own was dangerous.

That narrative completed the fracture.

Black men learned to stand alone—not out of pride, but out of conditioning. Brotherhood became symbolic instead of practical. Trust was limited. Collaboration was rare.

"I'm not my brother's keeper" became a survival creed.

COINTELPRO perfected this fracture.

The FBI and other agencies didn't just infiltrate organizations— they weaponized distrust. Informants were groomed. Leaders were betrayed. Brothers sold out brothers for safety, money, or survival.

William O'Neal's betrayal of Fred Hampton was not an anomaly. It was the continuation of a method refined over centuries. Black men were incentivized, coerced, or manipulated into destroying their own leadership from the inside.

Malcolm X did not fall to an outside enemy alone.
The Panthers did not collapse solely from external pressure.

Distrust did the work.

This chapter is not about condemnation. It is about recognition.

Black men were not born unwilling to protect each other. We were trained to believe that proximity to each other was dangerous. That trust would get us killed, incarcerated, or stripped of opportunity.

So, we adapted.

We learned to move alone.
To guard our ideas.
To keep distance.
To treat brotherhood as slogan instead of structure.

The cost of that adaptation has been enormous.

Without trust, we cannot build.
Without unity, we cannot protect.
Without shared ownership, wealth evaporates.

This chapter matters because rebuilding manhood requires confronting this fracture honestly. It requires recognizing that distrust among Black men did not emerge organically. It was engineered.

And what was engineered can be unlearned.

But only if we're willing to name it.

CHAPTER 28

The Collapse

Collapse rarely announces itself.

It does not arrive as explosion or spectacle.
It arrives as exhaustion—accumulated, normalized, and ignored until it can no longer be carried.

For Black men, collapse has historically been framed as personal failure.
In reality, it has been the predictable outcome of sustained structural pressure applied across generations.

By the late twentieth century, the conditions were set.

Political power had been stripped.
Economic access had been contained.
Leadership had been targeted and dismantled.
Fatherhood had been destabilized.
Legitimate reentry had been obstructed.

What remained was endurance without relief.

Black men were expected to absorb stress without outlet. To adapt continuously without rest. To survive conditions that shifted faster than any one man could recalibrate. Collapse was not the result of weakness—it was the cost of prolonged adaptation.

This phase did not begin when a man stopped working.
It began while he was still showing up.

Men remained employed—often precariously.
They remained present—often unofficially.
They remained functional—until function itself became unsustainable.

The strategies that once preserved survival began to erode stability.

Silence stopped protecting and started isolating.
Hustle stopped motivating and started draining.
Control stopped stabilizing and started suffocating.

These were not emotional failures.
They were system failures manifesting internally.

When effort no longer produces progress, the nervous system recalibrates. A man becomes vigilant, guarded, and reactive. Over time, this state hardens into chronic strain.

Sleep does not restore it.
Achievement does not resolve it.
Discipline does not cure it.

This is how collapse occurs without collapse appearing.

Historically, Black men have been denied recovery periods afforded to other populations. After wars, recessions, and social upheavals, relief programs and institutional forgiveness were selectively applied. For Black men, punishment often followed disruption instead of support.

So, pressure stacked.

Each generation inherited unresolved stress from the one before it. Coping strategies were passed down without explanation. Endurance became identity. Vulnerability became risk.

Eventually, the body intervenes.

The collapse is not always dramatic. It may present as withdrawal. As irritability. As disengagement. As sudden loss of motivation. As inability to maintain emotional presence. As internal shutdown.

This is not breakdown in the clinical sense.
It is overload.

The collapse exposes a critical truth: survival mechanisms have limits. Systems designed to endure oppression are not designed to sustain wholeness.

When collapse arrives, it forces stillness—not by choice, but by failure of function.

Productivity no longer numbs.
Distraction no longer works.
Motion no longer outruns the questions.

At this point, a man is often told to "get help" without acknowledgment of what broke him. Therapy is offered without context. Accountability is demanded without repair.

This misdiagnosis deepens the collapse.

The truth is simpler and harder.

Black men did not collapse because they were unprepared for life.
They collapsed because they were required to carry what no individual was meant to carry alone.

The collapse reveals what systems refused to hold.

It exposes the difference between strength and strain.
Between endurance and sustainability.
Between functioning and living.

This chapter marks the moment when survival strategies turn inward.

Not as rebellion.
Not as weakness.
But as consequence.

And once that collapse occurs, returning to "how things were" is no longer possible.

Something has been exposed.

Something has failed.

And something—if addressed honestly—can finally change.

CHAPTER 29

Sitting With Myself

After collapse, movement loses its power.

For generations, Black men were conditioned to stay in motion. Work harder. Push through. Adjust. Endure. Stillness was treated as danger—because historically, stillness made a man visible, and visibility carried risk.

So, motion became safety.

But once collapse interrupts that motion, a man is left with something unfamiliar: uninterrupted presence.

Sitting with oneself is not a therapeutic exercise by default. For Black men, it has often been historically unsafe. Stillness meant exposure—to law enforcement, to surveillance, to suspicion, to internal reckoning without tools.

This is why sitting with oneself feels threatening.

When external pressure temporarily lifts—or when the body can no longer respond—the absence of motion reveals what endurance had been suppressing.

Unprocessed grief.
Deferred anger.
Internalized fear.
Inherited silence.

None of these originate in the moment. They accumulate across time.

The absence of distraction removes the scaffolding that survival required. Without constant engagement, the nervous system begins to surface unresolved material. This is not psychological weakness. It is delayed processing.

For Black men, emotional processing was historically unsafe. Expressing fear invited exploitation. Expressing anger invited violence. Expressing sadness invited ridicule or dismissal. Over time, emotional containment became a survival skill.

Sitting with oneself dismantles that containment.

This is where discomfort emerges—not because something new is wrong, but because something old has finally lost its restraints.

Modern frameworks often misinterpret this phase as depression, laziness, or disengagement. In reality, it is recalibration. The mind is no longer braced against constant threat, and it does not yet know how to rest.

Questions surface without immediate answers.

Who am I without constant pressure?
Who am I when usefulness is not my justification?
Who am I outside survival?

Historically, Black men were valued for labor, endurance, and compliance—not introspection. There were few sanctioned spaces for self-reflection unconnected to productivity or punishment.

So, when stillness arrives, it feels unstructured.

Sitting with oneself also reveals how identity was shaped by necessity rather than choice. Many behaviors once labeled "personality" were actually adaptations to unstable environments.

Hyper-independence.
Emotional restraint.
Control.
Distance.

These traits were not chosen freely. They were selected under pressure.

Stillness exposes that truth.

This is often where men experience internal conflict. The survival identity resists dissolution. It warns against vulnerability. It urges movement, distraction, or re-engagement—even when exhaustion persists.

But sitting with oneself interrupts the reflex.

It creates a pause long enough for recognition.

Recognition that endurance was mistaken for strength.
Recognition that silence was mistaken for stability.
Recognition that independence was mistaken for freedom.

This stage does not provide resolution. It provides orientation.

A man begins to locate himself internally instead of externally. Instead of defining worth through output, he begins to observe capacity. Instead of reacting to pressure, he starts identifying thresholds.

Historically, Black men were denied this internal orientation. Their lives were shaped by external control—laws, patrols, policies, institutions. Sitting with oneself reclaims internal authority without confrontation.

This is not retreat.

It is recalibration.

The ability to sit without fleeing is a prerequisite for rebuilding. Without it, men simply re-enter the same cycles under different conditions.

Stillness becomes diagnostic.

It reveals what was learned under coercion.
What was carried without consent.
What no longer fits the current environment.

This chapter does not mark healing.

It marks awareness.

And awareness is the first point at which choice becomes possible again.

Once a man can sit with himself without panic, distraction, or collapse, he can begin the next phase—not survival, but intentional movement.

Not reaction, but direction.

CHAPTER 30

Learning to Feel Without Fleeing

Feeling was never the problem.

Avoidance wasn't either—at least not at first.

Survival was.

For most of my life, I did not live in a state of running.
I lived in a state of *standing*.

I stood in rooms where tension was thick.
I stood in relationships when things got hard.
I stood in responsibility long before I understood myself.

Like many Black men of my era, leaving was not always the instinct.
Often, staying was.

When pressure rose, I did not immediately disappear.
I reached for my partner.
I leaned into togetherness.
I believed—sometimes desperately—that if we stayed connected, we could figure it out.

That belief wasn't weakness.
It was hope trained by necessity.

We were raised to endure.
To push through.
To fight for what mattered.

And fight we did.

Black men were never taught to be passive.
We were taught to resist.

We learned to fight back when disrespected.
To stand our ground when challenged.
To protect when threatened.

Sometimes that fight showed up as confrontation.
Sometimes as anger.
Sometimes as silence held like armor.

And sometimes, when the pressure had no release valve, we created.

We sang.
We danced.
We wrote.
We built rhythm where there was no peace.
We found ways to *move pain through the body* when the world gave us no language for it.

That was not fleeing.

That was expression.

But expression is not the same as integration.

Over time, I began to realize something uncomfortable:

I could stand in the storm
and still not know what to do with what I was feeling.

I could fight outwardly
and still be lost internally.

I could stay in relationships
and still be emotionally disoriented.

The issue was not courage.
It was instruction.

No one had taught me how to stay present inside discomfort without turning it into action, reaction, or performance.

When feelings surfaced—fear, grief, disappointment—my nervous system looked for movement.

Not always escape.

Sometimes confrontation.
Sometimes productivity.
Sometimes logic.
Sometimes control.

Work harder.
Think faster.
Fix something.
Say something sharp.
Hold it together.

Anything that prevented stillness.

Because stillness felt dangerous.

Stillness meant there was nothing to *do* with the feeling.

So even when I stayed physically, I often fled emotionally.

That distinction matters.

Learning to feel without fleeing did not mean learning to leave less.
It meant learning to remain internally when there was nothing left to fight.

My body had been trained by generations of pressure to treat discomfort as threat.
When emotion stirred, my system looked for exits—or weapons.

Work.
Movement.
Argument.
Control.
Silence.

Anything but being with it.

So, I had to learn a new skill.

Not bravery.
Not toughness.

Presence.

Instead of immediately acting on discomfort, I began asking
what it was asking for.
Instead of labeling emotions as weakness or strength, I treated
them as information.
Instead of trying to win the moment, I tried to understand it.

That felt unnatural.

Fear, especially, had always been something to overcome or
suppress.
But I learned that fear is not the enemy.

Fear is a signal.
It tells you where something matters.
Where attachment exists.
Where loss is possible.

Fighting fear doesn't eliminate it.
Ignoring fear doesn't erase it.

It just drives it underground.

And buried fear hardens.

Grief was even harder.

Grief doesn't want strategy.
It doesn't want productivity.
It doesn't want resolution.

It wants space.

I had losses I never paused to mourn.
Relationships I "moved on" from without honoring what they cost.
Versions of myself I abandoned because survival demanded it.

Those things don't disappear.

They wait.

Learning to feel meant letting grief surface without minimizing it.
Without comparing it.
Without telling myself I should be stronger because I'd survived worse.

Pain is not a competition.

Allowing myself to feel sadness without turning it into anger or motion did not weaken me.

It grounded me.

My reactions softened.
My responses slowed.
My presence deepened.

Emotions stopped ambushing me because I was no longer avoiding them.

Anger changed too.

I had always respected anger's power—and feared it.
I associated it with danger, escalation, loss of control.

So, I learned to manage it tightly or channel it outward.

But anger, when listened to, was rarely the problem.

It was guarding something else.

Boundaries.
Disappointment.

Violation.
Unmet needs.

Learning to feel anger without fleeing meant listening instead of exploding.
Naming instead of performing.
Responding instead of reacting.

This took practice.

And patience.

There were still moments I fought when I should have paused.
Moments I withdrew when I should have spoken.

Healing is not linear.

But something fundamental shifted.

I stopped seeing emotion as something to defeat.
I stopped seeing stillness as weakness.
I stopped seeing vulnerability as surrender.

I learned that staying does not always mean holding on.
Sometimes it means staying with yourself long enough to understand what is actually happening.

That changed how I showed up.

I spoke sooner.
I clarified instead of hardening.
I asked for reassurance instead of assuming abandonment.
I named discomfort instead of carrying it alone.

Learning to feel without fleeing did not make life easier.

It made it truer.

And truth—real truth—creates stability that endurance alone never could.

For the first time, I wasn't just surviving my emotions.

I was standing inside them.

And learning from them.

CHAPTER 31

Forgiveness Is Not Forgetting

Forgiveness has been misunderstood—deliberately.

For Black men, forgiveness has often been framed as compliance. As silence. As moving on without acknowledgment. As absorbing harm in the name of peace while systems remain unchanged.

That version of forgiveness is not healing.

It is erasure.

Forgiveness is not the removal of memory.
It is the removal of captivity.

Forgetting asks a man to abandon evidence. Forgiveness allows a man to release the emotional hold of injury without surrendering truth. The distinction matters because forgetting repeats harm, while forgiveness interrupts it.

Historically, Black men were pressured to forgive without justice. To reconcile without repair. To demonstrate restraint while injuries accumulated. This created a false binary: either hold resentment or accept abuse.

There is a third path.

Forgiveness without forgetting is that path.

It begins internally.

Before a man can forgive others, he must confront the weight of self-blame produced by survival. Many Black men were taught—implicitly and explicitly—that failure to thrive was personal. That endurance should have been enough. That resilience should have compensated for exclusion.

It did not.

Forgiving oneself means acknowledging limited options without excusing harm. It means recognizing that survival strategies were chosen under constraint. That tools were inherited, not designed freely.

This does not erase accountability.

It restores context.

Context changes how responsibility is carried. It allows growth without self-contempt. It replaces shame with clarity.

From there, forgiveness moves outward.

This does not require minimizing harm done by others. It requires understanding how harm is often transmitted through systems before it appears in relationships. Fathers passed down silence learned under threat. Institutions normalized exclusion behind procedure. Individuals enacted roles shaped by pressure.

Understanding this does not absolve behavior.

It locates it.

Forgiveness without forgetting allows a man to say: *What happened was real. The damage was real. And I will not carry it forward as resentment.*

Resentment is costly.

It anchors the nervous system to past injury. It narrows perception. It distorts present relationships by filtering them through old wounds. Over time, it becomes a form of self-surveillance—constant, exhausting, and unproductive.

Forgiveness disrupts that loop.

It releases emotional ownership of harm without surrendering boundaries.

This is where forgiveness is most often confused with reconciliation.

They are not the same.

Reconciliation requires safety, accountability, and change. Forgiveness does not. Forgiveness is unilateral. It can occur without acknowledgment, apology, or repair from the other party.

Waiting for permission to heal is another form of captivity.

Forgetting, by contrast, is dangerous.

Forgetting removes pattern recognition. It erases warning signs. It invites repetition under new names. Systems rely on forgetting to preserve themselves.

Memory protects.

Forgiveness without forgetting allows a man to remember clearly without reliving continuously. To hold truth without bleeding into new situations. To respond rather than react.

This reorientation reshapes conflict.

Not every disagreement becomes a reenactment of past harm. Not every rupture signals abandonment. Not every mistake requires withdrawal or escalation.

Perspective expands.

Forgiveness also recalibrates masculinity. It reframes strength away from emotional hardness and toward emotional sovereignty. A man who can release resentment without denial is not weak.

He is free.

Historically, Black men were taught to endure injustice quietly or explode under pressure. Forgiveness without forgetting offers a third option: clarity with restraint.

This chapter does not argue for peace at any cost.

It argues for peace with memory intact.

Because forgetting enables repetition.
And resentment enables stagnation.

Forgiveness—properly understood—creates movement.

It allows a man to step forward without dragging old injuries behind him. To protect himself without hardening. To remember without being ruled by memory.

Forgiveness is not forgetting.

It is choosing not to let past wounds dictate future posture.

That choice restores agency.

And agency—not amnesia—is what healing requires.

CHAPTER 32

Rebuilding Manhood

Rebuilding manhood does not begin with instruction.
It begins with recognition.

Before a man can build something durable, he must understand what he has been standing on. For Black men in America, much of what is labeled masculinity was not freely chosen. It was shaped under pressure—by surveillance, exclusion, punishment, and absence.

This distinction matters.

What looks like identity is often adaptation.
What looks like personality is often survival.

Historically, Black masculinity was forced into narrow lanes. Strength was demanded, but leadership was punished. Provision was expected, but access was denied. Emotional restraint was rewarded, but emotional expression was treated as liability. Over time, these contradictions hardened into behavior.

Rebuilding requires separating what was *necessary* from what is *healthy*.

Manhood, before interruption, was never meant to be a performance. It was a role reinforced by community, accountability, and continuity. In America, those supports were deliberately dismantled. What remained was endurance without instruction.

Endurance alone is not manhood.
It is capacity under strain.

Rebuilding manhood means reintroducing elements that were systematically removed.

First: presence.
Not visibility. Presence.

A present man is not merely physically nearby. He is emotionally accessible, psychologically grounded, and accountable to impact. Historically, Black men were conditioned to reduce presence to avoid danger. Withdrawal became safety. Silence became strategy.

That strategy protected bodies.
It did not build families.

Rebuilding requires redefining presence as strength rather than risk.

Second: language.
Manhood without language becomes volatility.

Black men were taught to act without explaining, to carry without naming, to endure without processing. This produced competence without communication. Function without intimacy. Leadership without translation.

Rebuilding manhood means developing emotional and relational literacy—not as softness, but as precision. A man who can name his internal state is less reactive, more stable, and harder to manipulate.

Language creates regulation.
Regulation creates safety.

Third: accountability with context.
Accountability divorced from history becomes punishment.

Black men have been held responsible for outcomes while denied access to inputs. Rebuilding does not reject accountability—it reframes it. Responsibility begins where agency exists. Awareness creates obligation, but obligation must be paired with opportunity.

This prevents the internalization of shame.

Shame immobilizes.
Responsibility mobilizes.

Fourth: community.
Manhood does not mature in isolation.

The removal of the village forced men into solitary survival. Independence became virtue because dependence was dangerous. Over time, isolation was mistaken for strength.

Rebuilding requires reintroducing safe male reflection—spaces where men can be seen without competition, corrected without humiliation, and held accountable without threat.

This is not nostalgia.
It is infrastructure.

Fifth: integration.
Rebuilding does not erase the past. It integrates it.

A man does not honor his father by repeating unfinished patterns. He honors him by completing what was interrupted. This is not rejection of masculinity—it is refinement.

Strength remains.
Discipline remains.
Provision remains.

What changes is scope.

Manhood expands to include emotional regulation, relational responsibility, and internal alignment. A rebuilt man can endure *and* feel. Lead *and* listen. Provide *and* be present.

This is not theoretical.

Men raised without modeling improvise masculinity. Improvisation under trauma produces inconsistency. Rebuilding replaces improvisation with intention.

That intention reshapes outcomes.

Rebuilt manhood stabilizes families.
It reduces reactivity.
It interrupts generational fracture.

This chapter is not a conclusion.
It is a direction.

Rebuilding manhood is not a destination reached once. It is a practice maintained deliberately—against pressure, against history, and against systems that still benefit from fragmentation.

But for the first time, the work is conscious.

And conscious reconstruction is the opposite of survival.

It is authorship.

CHAPTER 33

Becoming Present

Presence was never encouraged.
It was survived around.

For most of American history, Black men learned that visibility carried risk. To be seen too clearly was to invite scrutiny. To be heard too clearly was to invite punishment. To stand too firmly was to be marked.

So, men adapted.

They learned how to be physically present while emotionally guarded. How to provide without explaining. How to endure without engaging. Presence became proximity, not participation.

This was not neglect.
It was conditioning.

Becoming present requires undoing that conditioning.

Presence is not passivity.
It is regulation.

A present man is not reactive. He is responsive. He does not disappear under pressure or dominate to regain control. He stays engaged long enough to influence outcomes rather than merely survive them.

Historically, Black men were denied the safety required for that kind of engagement. Jim Crow punished confidence. Policing criminalized assertion. Workplaces penalized emotional expression. Homes were destabilized by forced absence.

Over time, detachment became protection.

But protection has a cost.

When a man is not fully present, relationships become unstable. Children experience availability without access. Partners experience effort without intimacy. Communities experience labor without leadership.

Becoming present means closing that gap.

This does not happen through intention alone. It requires skills that were never taught.

Emotional regulation is one of them.

Black men were often socialized to suppress emotion rather than process it. Anger was dangerous. Sadness was weakness. Fear was unacceptable. The safest option was neutrality.

Neutrality looks calm.
Internally, it is tension.

Presence requires the ability to feel without fleeing, to name discomfort without escalation, and to remain engaged even when outcomes are uncertain. These are learned capacities—not personality traits.

Another requirement is trust.

You cannot be present where you expect harm.

Generations of Black men learned to anticipate misinterpretation. To assume their words would be used against them. To believe that vulnerability invited exploitation. This trained men to stay partially hidden—even with those they loved.

Becoming present requires recalibrating threat assessment.

Not every disagreement is danger.
Not every misunderstanding is abandonment.
Not every pause requires withdrawal.

This recalibration is work.

Presence also requires consistency.

In unstable environments, inconsistency is adaptive. You show up when it's safe. You retreat when it's not. Over time, this produces intermittent presence—unpredictable, fragmented, and confusing to others.

Children experience this as absence even when a man is trying.

Becoming present means choosing reliability over reflex. It means showing up emotionally as consistently as physically. It means being reachable—not perfect.

Presence is not grand gesture.
It is repetition.

There is also a political dimension to presence.

A present Black man contradicts long-standing narratives. He disrupts assumptions about disengagement, irresponsibility, and emotional distance. This disruption has historically been punished.

That punishment trained caution.

But absence does not protect indefinitely.
It only delays cost.

Becoming present is an act of resistance—not loud, but durable. It rebuilds trust at the scale where systems have always been weakest: the relational level.

Fathers become present.
Partners become present.
Men become present with themselves.

This presence stabilizes identity.

A man who is present knows what he feels, why he feels it, and how to communicate it without collapse. He does not need to disappear to stay safe. He does not need dominance to feel in control.

He is grounded.

This chapter matters because rebuilding manhood without presence is cosmetic. It changes language but not outcomes. Presence is where theory becomes lived reality.

Becoming present does not erase history.
It corrects trajectory.

And when enough men choose presence over protection, the inherited pattern breaks—not through confrontation, but through consistency.

That is how reconstruction holds.

CHAPTER 34

What I Teach Now

What I teach now is not theory.
It is consequence.

It is built from patterns observed across history, policy, and lived outcome—not from opinion or reaction. Every lesson I pass forward is shaped by what has repeatedly worked against Black men and what has consistently been withheld from them.

The first lesson is context.

I teach that behavior does not appear in a vacuum. Black men are often judged as if they were self-generated—untethered from history, policy, or environment. That framing is false. Every major pattern in Black male life can be traced to specific decisions, laws, and enforcement mechanisms.

Understanding context is not about excusing behavior.
It is about locating cause.

Without context, accountability becomes punishment.
With context, accountability becomes direction.

The second lesson is alignment.

I teach that effort without access is not failure—it is misalignment. For generations, Black men were told to work harder inside systems designed to deny return. This produced exhaustion, cynicism, and disengagement.

Alignment means matching effort to pathways that actually yield outcome. It means learning how systems function—not idealistically, but operationally. It means recognizing when persistence is required and when redirection is necessary.

This is not bitterness.
It is literacy.

The third lesson is structure.

I teach that discipline without structure collapses. Motivation without systems burns out. Black men were trained to endure without being taught how to organize endurance into sustainability.

Structure includes routines, financial frameworks, emotional regulation practices, and community accountability. These are not personality traits. They are learned systems.

Structure reduces volatility.
Structure preserves energy.

The fourth lesson is emotional competence.

Historically, Black men were punished for emotional expression and penalized for vulnerability. This produced silence, not strength. Emotional competence is not emotional exposure—it is emotional management.

I teach men how to identify internal states, regulate response, and communicate clearly without escalation or withdrawal. This skill is critical in relationships, workplaces, and parenting.

A man who cannot regulate emotion is easy to provoke.
A man who can is difficult to control.

The fifth lesson is ownership.

Ownership is not limited to property. It includes ownership of time, narrative, decision-making, and consequence. Black men were repeatedly positioned as labor without authority, output without control.

I teach men to prioritize ownership wherever possible—skills that transfer, assets that appreciate, knowledge that compounds. Not because wealth is moral, but because dependency is dangerous.

Ownership creates leverage.
Leverage creates choice.

The sixth lesson is discernment.

Not every opportunity is opportunity. Not every ally is aligned. Black men were historically targeted through false access—contracts, partnerships, and assistance that extracted value without protection.

Discernment is the ability to slow down decisions, evaluate incentives, and recognize imbalance before commitment. This skill was never formally taught—but its absence has been costly.

Speed benefits systems.
Discernment protects people.

The seventh lesson is presence with purpose.

Visibility without strategy invites harm. Invisibility without intention creates erasure. I teach men how to be present where it matters—family, craft, community—without overexposing themselves to unnecessary risk.

This is not fear.
It is precision.

Presence is most powerful when it is consistent, grounded, and deliberate.

Finally, I teach completion.

Black men are not required to reject their fathers, ancestors, or history to evolve. They are required to complete what was interrupted. To carry forward strength while adding what was denied—language, reflection, and emotional literacy.

Completion honors lineage.
Repetition does not.

What I teach now is not designed to make Black men acceptable. It is designed to make them whole, strategic, and durable in environments that were never built for their stability.

This is not inspiration.
It is instruction.

And instruction—when grounded in truth—is how interruption ends.

CHAPTER 35

Going Home

Going home is not a return to a place.
It is a return to alignment.

For Black men, "home" has been treated as a contradiction—
something sentimental rather than structural. But home was
never just shelter. It was authority, continuity, and grounding.
And its removal was never accidental.

To understand going home, you have to understand what was
taken.

Black men were removed from land.
Removed from family authority.
Removed from political voice.
Removed from economic pathways.
Removed from leadership roles.
Removed from safety.

Then told to rebuild without access.

Going home does not mean nostalgia for a past that cannot be
recreated. It means reclaiming the functions that were
deliberately interrupted—and rebuilding them in the present with
clarity.

The first return is to self-definition.

For centuries, Black men were defined by others—by law, by
policy, by media, by enforcement. Identity was imposed.
Deviation was punished.

Going home begins when a man defines himself internally instead of reacting externally. When his decisions are guided by intention rather than pressure. When his value is not negotiated through compliance.

A man who defines himself is difficult to displace.

The second return is to responsibility without erasure.

Responsibility has often been demanded from Black men without authority, without protection, and without reward. That version of responsibility was extraction.

Going home means reclaiming responsibility as agency— choosing what to carry, what to build, and what to refuse. It means rejecting the lie that responsibility requires self-sacrifice without return.

True responsibility includes sustainability.

The third return is to lineage.

Lineage is not worship of ancestors. It is understanding sequence. Knowing what was passed down intact, what was damaged, and what was never delivered.

Black men were not born broken. They were interrupted.

Going home means completing the transfer. Carrying forward endurance while adding reflection. Carrying forward strength while adding emotional regulation. Carrying forward loyalty while adding discernment.

Lineage heals through completion, not repetition.

The fourth return is to presence.

Absence was engineered. Presence was criminalized. Visibility was punished. Silence became survival.

Going home means becoming present intentionally—in family, in craft, in community—without apology and without recklessness. Presence does not mean overexposure. It means consistency.

A present man changes outcomes quietly.

The fifth return is to ownership.

Home without ownership is temporary. Black men were historically allowed to labor but denied control. That imbalance created dependence and instability.

Going home means prioritizing ownership of skill, time, narrative, and asset wherever possible. Not as material obsession—but as protection.

Ownership reduces vulnerability.

The sixth return is to brotherhood with discernment.

Trust among Black men was fractured by design. Informants were incentivized. Competition was engineered. Unity was punished.

Going home does not mean blind trust. It means intentional collaboration—earned trust, shared standards, and mutual accountability.

Brotherhood is not automatic.
It is built.

The final return is to peace.

Peace is not passivity. It is regulation. It is the absence of
constant threat response. Black men were conditioned to live
braced—hypervigilant, reactive, guarded.

Going home means learning to stand down without becoming
vulnerable to harm. It means developing internal calm that is not
dependent on external approval.

A regulated man is not easily provoked.
A regulated man is not easily controlled.

This book was never about blaming individuals.
It was about exposing systems.

It was never about excusing behavior.
It was about identifying cause.

And it was never about despair.
It was about direction.

Going home is not symbolic.
It is practical.

It happens every time a Black man chooses alignment over
reaction. Structure over chaos. Ownership over dependence.
Presence over disappearance.

The interruption was intentional.
But it was not permanent.

What was engineered can be understood.
What is understood can be interrupted.
And what is interrupted can be rebuilt—deliberately.

Going home is how that rebuilding begins.

Not behind us.
Not ahead of us.

Within reach.

A Letter to Black Sons and Brothers

My sons and Brothers,

This is not a speech.

This is not poetry.

This is not a fantasy.

This is your inheritance.

You were not born broken.
You were not born dangerous.
You were not born disposable.

You were born with memory in your blood and strength in your bones.

Even if the world tried to rewrite your reflection, there is a blueprint inside you that cannot be erased. It predates this country. It predates your pain. It predates the systems designed to shrink you.

And it is waking up.

You are growing up in a world that studies you before it sees you. That fears you before it knows you. That profiles you before it understands you. But I need you to know this with clarity:

You were not created by their fear.
You were created by your lineage.

Your ancestors were not weak men.
They were disciplined men.
Structured men.
Men who knew who they were before they were forced to forget.

That memory did not leave your body.

It just went quiet.

This book was written so you could hear it again.

You will be told many lies about yourself.

That you are too emotional.
That you are too angry.
That you are too intense.
That you are too dangerous.
That you are too broken.

None of that is true.

What you are is carrying unspoken weight without instruction.

Nobody taught you how to lay it down.

So now I will.

You do not have to become a monster to be respected.
You do not have to become cold to be valuable.
You do not have to become numb to be strong.

You are allowed to feel and still be a man.
You are allowed to cry and still be powerful.
You are allowed to love deeply and still be dangerous — but

dangerous in the way a storm is dangerous, not in the way fire is chaotic.

Dangerous with discipline.
Dangerous with direction.
Dangerous with control.

You are not being asked to become soft.

You are being invited to become whole.

You will inherit anger that is not fully yours.
You will feel grief you cannot name.
You will carry mistrust that wasn't born in your lifetime.

That is not weakness.

That is history moving through you.

But history does not get to dictate your future.

You can feel it without becoming it.

Your job is not to impress the world.

Your job is to know yourself so deeply that the world cannot distort you.

You don't need permission to be intelligent.
You don't need validation to be calm.
You don't need fear to be respected.

You do not need chaos to feel alive.

I need you to understand this:
You were never meant to "make it out."

You were meant to build within.

You are allowed to love yourself without proving anything.
You are allowed to choose peace without being called weak.
You are allowed to hold your head steady without making noise.

You do not have to entertain stereotypes.
You do not have to carry every expectation.
You do not have to perform trauma.

You can be disciplined without cruelty.
Firm without violence.
Protective without domination.

That is your birthright.

You are not here to destroy.

You are here to stabilize.

You are not here to prove.

You are here to remember.

When you feel lost, do not search the world.

Search your silence.

Your home is not somewhere else.

Your home is where your thoughts slow down.

Your home is where your breath deepens.

Your home is where you don't feel hunted by yourself.

That is what "go home" means.

And when you get there, you don't keep it to yourself.

You show other men how to find it.

Not through speeches.

Through posture.

Through calm.

Through example.

Through presence.

Your existence is not a reaction to pain.

It is a continuation of strength.

This book ends here.

But your work does not.

You are not behind.
You are not late.
You are not confused.

You are waking up.

And that is the most dangerous thing you can do in a world built to keep you asleep.

Walk gently.

Stand firmly.

Breathe deeply.

And remember:

Your crown was never taken.

It was hidden.

And now you know where to look.

REFERENCES & SOURCES

Alexander, Michelle. *The New Jim Crow: Mass Incarceration in the Age of Colorblindness.* The New Press.

Anderson, Carol. *White Rage: The Unspoken Truth of Our Racial Divide.* Bloomsbury.

Blackmon, Douglas A. *Slavery by Another Name.* Anchor Books.

Bureau of Justice Statistics. *Prisoners in the United States.*

Coates, Ta-Nehisi. *Between the World and Me.* Spiegel & Grau.

Federal Bureau of Investigation. *COINTELPRO Records (1956–1971).*

Feagin, Joe R. *Systemic Racism: A Theory of Oppression.* Routledge.

Hinton, Elizabeth. *From the War on Poverty to the War on Crime.* Harvard University Press.

Kendi, Ibram X. *Stamped from the Beginning.* Nation Books.

Moynihan, Daniel Patrick. *The Negro Family: The Case for National Action.* U.S. Department of Labor.

National Archives. *Redlining Maps & HOLC Records.*

Nixon, Richard. *Special Message to the Congress on Drug Abuse Prevention and Control* (1971).

Ogletree, Charles J. *All Deliberate Speed.* W.W. Norton & Company.

United States Department of Housing and Urban Development. *History of Redlining.*

United States Congress. *GI Bill of Rights (Servicemen's Readjustment Act of 1944).*

Williams, Chad L. *Torchbearers of Democracy: African American Soldiers in the World War I Era.*

www.ingramcontent.com/pod-product-compliance
Lightning Source LLC
Chambersburg PA
CBHW031430270326
41930CB00007B/651